BECOMING THE

BRIDE OF CHRIST

BECOMING THE BRIDE OF CHRIST

A Personal Journey

Volume 1

by Marilynn Dawson

All Scripture quoted from the King James Version (Public Domain) unless otherwise stated.

ISBN 978-0-9881181-0-2

This book is dedicated to Everyone who has been there for me during the events that led me to the doorway of this new chapter in my faithwalk and beyond.

I first want to thank my Lord and Saviour Jesus Christ, God the Father, and God the Holy Spirit for each showing Himself true to the Scriptures He dictated to man, in how He made Himself so very real in my life and that of my children.

I wish to thank my parents who raised me in a Christian home, taught me to think critically, to always test the spirits, and imitate the Bereans in understanding the Word of God. I also wish to thank them and my siblings for being there when I found myself fleeing my marriage and the resulting trials that ensued.

I wish to thank the pastoral staff of Evangel Church in Kelowna BC Canada, for being there for me or my children in a variety of ways. Pr Don Hopkinson, Pr Kevin Draper, Pr Marty Mittelstaedt, Pr Will Sohnchen, Pr Phil Spoelstra, Pr Matt Jaggers and Pr Don Richmond. Each of these pastors, during their times in Pastoral Office at Evangel, had input into my life and/or my children's lives, and I thank you! Many of the lessons shared in this book would not have been learned if it weren't for your efforts and obedience to God's promptings.

This list wouldn't be complete if I didn't add two special online friends I've known since the early 2000's. Shalynn, or Shannon, and His Child, or Michele, took it upon themselves to assist with editing! No small task for the size of this book! Thank you from the bottom of my heart!

BECOMING THE BRIDE OF CHRIST

A Personal Journey

by Marilynn Dawson

Books in this Series:

Table of Contents

Chapter 1

Chapter 2

Chapter 3

Chapter 3 Cont. . .

Chapter 4

Chapter 4 Cont. . .

In a Time Long Ago. . . But More Recent Than I Wish to Admit. . . the Following Events Occurred. . .

I'd been avoiding a certain little hatchback for several days, each time leaving just as they arrived, or arriving as they pulled away down the street. I knew from voice messages left on my phone that this person needed to see me, however I didn't want to see them. But today hadn't been so lucky. . . The package had been delivered, signed for, and I was left standing in my little basement suite kitchen staring at papers suing me for divorce and custody of my two small children!

Secretly long-held fears flooded in as it dawned on me they were about to be realized. The biggest fear to clobber me at that moment was the prospect of becoming a single mother!

A visit to a local female lawyer revealed that failure to combat these papers would more than likely default victory to my estranged husband and hand him the kids in the process. If I wanted any hope of raising my children, I needed to counter-sue.

Counter-sue for divorce. . . Now more fears rose. . . Nightmares created by teachings from the pulpit heard from the pew as a small child. . . If I was to counter-sue for divorce, the nightmares shouted, I would lose any prospect of ever engaging in ministry in God's House! No more teaching Sunday School, no more singing on the praise teams, no more kids choir leadership, no more assistance in the office. . . This nightmare whispered that I would never minister again if I sued for divorce. . . And the trauma got worse. . .

Fleeing my husband had been traumatic as it was. I was raised that marriage was for life and I'd been trying for two years by that point to keep a failing 6 year old marriage together. My ex had said if anyone came for the kids to take them away, he'd meet them with a gun, of which he owned several. . . I had learned to clean, polish, disassemble and reassemble these things, and even how to aim and shoot them. . . This was the last straw in what had become an abusive relationship. The counsellors at the women's shelter to which a victim's assistance officer had brought us, identified several areas of abuse. . . financial, sexual, relational, social, and emotional. Fortunately physical abuse wasn't in the mix, but some of the other scars I swear cut deeper and hurt worse than physical wounds ever could! In fact I am convinced that physical wounds heal far quicker and more completely than those hidden from the naked eye.

Flight or fight syndrome had kept me going for two full weeks on extremely little sleep as I closed out accounts, wrapped up affairs at various venues and businesses around town, and prepared to get my children out of the province and back into my home province. The counsellors had never seen a woman try so methodically and deliberately to pull what pieces she could of her life together to start over. My sister made a kamikaze trip with a rented van to whisk my two small children and myself, and what few belongings we could grab from the house, out of that city! I wouldn't find out till 6 months later, that an hour after we crossed the provincial border, my ex had obtained a restraining order to keep my kids in Alberta! This piece of paper would never be produced in a court of law.

So here I was, three months into life back in British Columbia, struggling with the thought that not only had I fled a failed marriage, but I was now facing the prospect of never serving in my Lord's House again. I honestly don't know which was more traumatic, losing my marriage, or losing the ministerial giftings God had given me.

Finally I did it. . . I replaced the phone in its cradle and sat down at my desk, staring blankly into the rest of the living room. . . I'd begun the counter-sue. . . As the fall season began, I figured the one place I could still minister was in the choir. . . at least there it seemed few people asked questions and perhaps I could minister if no one knew what I was facing.

Those first three months had been a whirlwind of activity in spite of how tender my nerves were. Every minor confrontation would set my nerves to shaking like a leaf! I couldn't handle it. . . Yet I was putting myself through college to get a career to feed my children. I'd found my own place in that little basement suite. Found a car. Put my son back into kindergarten and my daughter into daycare. There was no room for tears, no room for emotional outbursts. . . Until the divorce proceedings began to jump into full swing. . .

Then it snowed. . . that particular day my lawyer seemed more upset than I was over how things were going between my ex and the lawyer he'd obtained.

Things were emotionally tense and my poor lawyer needed calming down more than I did. . . when I looked out the window and saw snow blanketing everything. . . That would be the first time I felt God's overwhelming, calming, reassuring peace. . . the first time I would solidly get the message that God had it all under control. . . There would be many more emotionally trying moments, days and weeks, and any time I would come to the end of my rope thinking I couldn't take a moment more, it would snow! Every single time dear reader. . . Right into the spring of the year 2000. As proceedings were winding down, God quelled another stressful and emotional moment with a late spring freak snowfall! I looked out my window and couldn't help laughing at the ludicrous timing of that blanket of snow near the end of March. I shook my head and prayed, asking God for a positive outcome to this nightmare.

The divorce would finalize by the end of June, early July of 2000, with the courts giving me custody of the children with no alimony or child support. For those who are curious, it was a result of calling my ex's bluff when he kept saying he couldn't afford child support throughout the divorce proceedings. When he was offered the chance to grant me full custody without child support, he signed the paper!!! I and anyone who knew me, was shocked! The judge had actually approved and my ex had actually signed!

Now I was truly on my own, two small children in tow, a personal reputation lying in so many shattered shards at my feet. . . Tears joined those shards. . . many tears. . . My education had wrapped up and I would begin life as a working single mother that fall.

There were things I was adamant about never letting into my thoughts or home however! I wasn't going to live off the welfare system for starters! My ex had insisted we live off the system while he went to college several times, tried to urge me to find work while pregnant twice, and sponged off the church the rest of the time between short stints at various jobs. So I was determined we would not sponge off the government or the church! That we would be as self-sufficient as possible, as responsible as possible, as upstanding as possible, that no one would have reason to look upon my household as leaches or lazy bums. I also determined that we wouldn't live on the street, that I would do whatever was necessary to keep a roof over our heads and food on the table!

I lived this way from that summer of 2000 until 2006 when the second biggest personal storm would explode in my face and send me on probably the harshest whirlwind I'd ever experienced! My parents were moving away. My ex was threatening me with possible court action again and challenging my morals with the kids. My son was having major issues in school and at home, and I was getting nowhere with the school leadership. All this kicked up between late September and October, and I found myself slipping into a depression. Offers of hope in conversation or circumstance turned into blinding trains bowling me over under their wheels so often that by the time December rolled around, I was scared to get excited for anything, fearful that if I got too happy over some development, that it would turn into a raging lion and tear me to shreds! I wept for an hour one Sunday afternoon before taking part in a massive Christmas performance as a gift to our city.

This storm continued into 2007. A three week lull whipped up into a fury as my son was expelled from school and a guy who feigned mentoring my son to get my hand instead, was kicked out of our lives.

But then the strangest thing happened. . . Hardly a week after kicking that guy out of our lives, and hardly two weeks after obeying God's prompting to put my kids into the public school (against all gut feelings and experiences), I was sitting at my desk at noon working a quiet shift for Your Tech Online when suddenly I was enveloped in such an incredible warmth that I thought I'd fall asleep on the spot! My head fell forward and I straightened up shaking my-self wondering what just happened! It was then that an unmistakable sensation came over me, as if God were holding me in a 360 degree embrace and saying, "NOW I can love you!" Fresh tears began to flow as I sat there soaking in a love I had never anticipated could ever flow from God to me.

I honestly had never learned that God could touch my emotions. I had never expected that God's love and talk of His Bride would be anything more than ethereal head knowledge found in the pages of Scripture. Needless to say I had to go diving through the Scriptures to make sure I hadn't suddenly snapped and fallen off the deep end.

What followed led to the lessons, discoveries and revelations found in this series!

* * *

Living as the Bride of Christ in the every-day world.
What does this mean and how does one live this out?

God started me on a journey back in 2007 that would begin to reveal answers to this question. Penetrating answers, difficult answers, challenging answers, but as I began to step into those answers, I began to experience an intimacy with God that I'd only heard others talk about before.

I am a worshipper. My favourite form of communication between me and God is in the lyric and in the music. It is 100% true that worship is far more than music, that true worship is in actuality, a lifestyle that cultivates nearness toward God in all that we say, think and do with everyone and everything around us. But when it comes to those moments of closeness, those moments of heart touching heart, of spirit touching spirit, some find this on a mountain top after a gruelling hike. Some find this in the end of a paintbrush, or in wet clay between their fingers. I find it in music, and in silence. Consequently, as you begin to travel this journey with me, you will see many references to song lyrics that touched me along the way.

There are many Scriptures along this journey as well, and it is by no means over! The fact I am putting it down in words is simply this author working out her understanding of what God has taken her through, and sharing it with you. This has and continues to be a very intimate journey, a very personal journey, but also quite the adventure, and full of surprises. Life as a Christian for this author has never been boring, but since March of 2007, that defining moment when God first enveloped me in a 360 degree hug and introduced Himself as my unseen Husband, the level of adventure has simply intensified.

Welcome to my journey, welcome into my heart, mind and spirit as I share with you things that perhaps you may have already known but never thought of in this light before. Or, perhaps you've never been exposed to the concepts and thought patterns in this series. Maybe you don't even know the

Heavenly Bridegroom, our Lord and Saviour Jesus Christ. Wherever you are, I pray there is something here you can grasp and take hold of.

One thing I want to make clear from the start, is that the concept of the Bride of Christ does not merely encompass the world of women here on earth. We are told in **Galatians 3:28**, "There is neither Jew nor Greek, there is neither bond nor free, there is neither male nor female: for ye are all one in Christ Jesus." This means that in the spiritual realm, when we stand before Christ, we are all the same. It is only in dealing with each other that there is gender, and that by design back in Genesis chapter 1. Therefore the Bride of Christ is made up of the Church, as explained in **Ephesians 5:22-23**. John the Baptist himself knew of the future Bride of Christ, in his answer to his disciples when Christ was seen baptizing as He began His ministry. In **John 3:29** we see John saying, "He that hath the bride is the bridegroom: but the friend of the bridegroom, which standeth and heareth him, rejoiceth greatly because of the bridegroom's voice: this my joy therefore is fulfilled."

The Church is the Bride of Christ. Men and women make up the Church, and therefore, make up the Bride of Christ. So this book isn't just for women. It is written by a woman, but I lost count of the number of men I began running into since March of 2007, who were on similar journeys to myself, who were wanting to go deeper into the heart of God and who were facing similar challenges and adventures along the way. Some of these men actually began their journey before I did. As King David's been described as having a bridal heart toward God, so also do the men I have met since this new chapter in my life opened.

The first thing we have to deal with in becoming the Bride of Christ, is settling the issue of the Cross, of sin, of blame, of responsibility, of perfection and holiness. It all starts at the Cross. I invite you into chapter 2 as we dive into our first controversial discussion. . . where it all starts!

Getting the Most out of this Series:

Before diving into chapter 2, let's get some housekeeping out of the way.

To get the best out of this series and to make reading it as smooth as possible, a few things will need to be kept in mind. Where possible, visual cues will be given as well.

First, this is a series written as a combination of teaching and journaled experience, with Scripture, songs, and inspiration from others liberally sprinkled throughout. This means that sometimes you will read exhortation and teaching. Other times you will read discoveries and revelations as if you were right there with me in the moment! Still other times the text may read like a letter or a prayer.

To mark the differences between some of these styles of communication:

1) Prayers will be preceded by "**A Prayer**" and ended with ***. This is because prayer for me is always open-ended.
2) Letters will be preceded by "**A Letter**" and ended with *** as there is no need to "sign off" in this book.
3) Scriptures will either be indented off to the right if they are quoted by themselves, or their references in bold if they are included among other text.

In this way it is my hope that you will get the best possible reading experience through this study.

Each chapter will begin with a story segment of usually no more than two or three pages, followed immediately by the chapter heading and the rest of the chapter itself broken into study sessions. Each session will end with a collection of Scriptures, topics and songs either referenced or alluded to in the text, and some questions to help you appropriate what you're reading into your own life.

Supplemental to these resources, I invite my reader to visit http://songdove.fa-ct.com/ . There you will find interactive Scripture references, videos containing lyrics to most of the songs listed at the end of each session, topics mentioned in each session, and more. Public domain lyrics will be included in their entirety at the end of each session they appear in.

God has brought these discoveries and revelations to me through several major sources:

1) Scripture, including a 2 year trip through the Psalms.
2) Music, written by a large number of authors encompassing modern and older choruses, choir songs from the '80's to present, songs by various recording artists, and ancient as well as modern hymns.
3) "Song of Songs - Journey of the Bride" by Brian Simmons, available at: http://www.stairwayministries.org
4) "Living Beyond Yourself" by Beth Moore, a journey through the Fruit of the Spirit. http://www.lifeway.com/

If you wish to obtain these latter two resources for your own study, they are available online at their respective websites.

In addition to these top four sources, God also used a tabletop calendar from Focus on the Family called Daily Blessings, a Daily Bible Verse application on Facebook, sermons from my Senior Pastor, and numerous insights from my worship Pastor/Spiritual Mentor. You will see references to these sources in the text as well.

God speaks to us through many avenues if we will open our ears and eyes to receive them. I pray as you move forward in this study, that your spiritual eyes and ears will be opened to all the ways God wishes to engage in your life.

The last thing to note about the flow of text in this series, is that it is largely chronological! I have tried to separate out major themes into their respective chapters, but it hasn't been easy. It will be best to approach each chapter as occurring concurrently with or interspersed among all the other chapters.

Consequently there may be some repetition at times. I'll try to avoid this where possible, but it won't be completely unavoidable. You will come across phrases or paragraphs causing you to think, "Haven't I seen this somewhere before?". You more than likely have.

Explanation of Cover Art

When I first sat down to consider this project, it all looked like the visual equivalent of a tree with intertwining branches weaving in and around each other, hence the artwork on the front cover. It took a while to figure out how to present these lessons in a way that didn't boggle the reader and still offer that sense of discovery and revelation as it came to me. What you have in your hands is the result. The presentation isn't perfect by any means, but I pray it encourages you down your own path into the depths of God's heart.

To read Scriptures referenced in this chapter,
please visit http://songdove.fa-ct.com/
There you will find interactive Scripture references, videos containing lyrics to most of the songs in these chapters, topics mentioned in this chapter, and more.

Scriptures used, referred to or that relate to thoughts in this chapter:

Galatians 3:28   Ephesians 5:22-23   John 3:29

Questions for Discussion:

How would you describe your life in one or two short sentences?

_____

_____

What kind of a worshipper are you? _____

_____

Have you ever had a defining moment in your walk of faith?
YES___NO _____

If Yes, want to share a little?

_____

Have you accepted Christ as Lord and Saviour of your life?

YES_____ NO _____ If Yes, when did you get saved?

_____

 If No, what has drawn you to read this book?

_____

Now take a moment to reflect on what has made you pick up this book. What draws you to this topic? What is it you are hoping to gain from joining me on this journey? Write down your thoughts.

_____

_____

_____

In a Land, Far, Far away. . . But Closer than Any of Us Realize. . . the Following Story Began. . .

Everywhere you looked across the expansive room that served as meeting hall, banquet room, and court for the kindest King the realm had ever known, groups of people milled about, some in heated debates, others sharing animatedly, still other groups involved in signatory ceremony over trade of land or goods. Overlooking the buzz of activity from his seat at the far end of the room was the Great King Himself. He'd ruled this land for many years and now his Son, the Crown Prince, joined him at his side.

Together they scanned the crowds below. Most of the people within the court wore white in an amazing array of shapes and sizes. But occasionally an individual dressed in black could be seen weaving among the people. It puzzled some, why the Great and Kind King would allow these black-clad men into the palace, let alone the very seat of business on the floor of the court. But no one questioned Him.

Suddenly one of the men in black caught the gaze of the Crown Prince and His countenance grew pensive. The Crown Prince watched as this black-clad man quickened his pace through the throngs, weaving his way until he joined a group of similarly dressed men in a shadowy corner of the room. Agitated conversation ensued followed by the group quickly exiting the great hall.

Immediately the Crown Prince called for guards to follow them and report back! At the age of 30, the Crown Prince had never left the walls of the palace for much more than the occasional trip through the town market place, and His annual appearance at the Parade of the Realm. But He was starting to hear rumours of dissent among the peasants outside the Capital City, rumours of fear-mongering between the black guard and the farmers. He'd noticed more of them showing up in the court of late, and now he had to find out why!

Knowing His Son's thoughts, the Great King grabbed the Son's hand and beckoned Him to sit down again. "Son", He said quietly, "I fear that if you go after them that they will kill you and seek to take over the Kingdom."

The Son was about to protest, but the Great King continued. "There is but one way to purge the Realm of the black guard, and that is for them, and all they have won to their side, to die!"

At that, the Crown Prince rose up and hurried from the great hall! He called for the stable boy to ready His horse as he ran to the cloak room to change. He emerged just as a black guard walked past. Mistaking the Crown Prince for a peasant, the black guard sought to persuade the Son to join them in taking over the Realm, that they'd already converted vast areas of the countryside and now all they needed was to win the Capital City to dethrone the King.

The Crown Prince listened with intense interest, but held His peace. When the black guard realized he would get no response from this man, he went on his way. Once the black guard was out of sight, the Prince dashed to the royal stable and greeted his personal steed. Swift Wind nickered in return nuzzling the Crown Prince as He inspected the saddle and reigns. Satisfied that Swift Wind had been properly groomed and tacked up, the Crown Prince swung up into the saddle and rode out to the countryside.

The guards He sent to chase after the black-clad group came riding up and the Crown Prince greeted them. "Sir, "one palace guard began, "the hillsides are covered in black. If something isn't done and done soon, the Great King will lose all that he has worked so hard for among His people. The land must be purged or there will be nothing left!" Just then, another horse rode up. Everyone gasped as they realized who it was without body guards, soldiers, or even His own private entourage. The men backed up their horses to make room as the Great King Himself rode into their midst.

"Father, what are you going to do?" The Crown Prince asked.

"My Son. . . " The Great King responded as He gazed around the hills and meadows, "It is time. . . There is only one way to purge the land of this darkness. Every person who has chosen the way of black instead of white, must die."

"But Father, surely there must be another way. Let me go to these people, to our people, and show them once again how they may live white lives pleasing in your sight. Let me win them back. I love them Father. If you kill every black-clad peasant, who will be left?"

The Great King's face furrowed as He stroked His flowing white beard. "Son, they will kill you. They do not know you the way the city folk do. They will beat you and strip you and hang you up to die like a petty criminal."

"Let me go Father! And should they kill me, may it be in your sight as if every black-clad man, woman, and child of the Realm had died with me. Let them find life in my death."

The Great King's questioning eyes rose and rested on the Crown Prince's face. "Are you willing to do this thing? Are you willing to give your life to spare the lives of every living soul across the Realm?"

The Crown Prince nodded. "Yes Father, I am willing."

The Great King turned His horse about to return in the direction from which He'd come. "Then know this my Son. . . After you have paid the price in full, You will be welcome at my side once more. But be aware, the moment they hang you above the earth, I must turn my back. It will be too much for me to look upon my own Son bearing the insult, the rebellion, and the colour of all that is evil."

The Crown Prince's visage turned grey as He nodded in affirmation. "Yes Father, I understand. Now let me go. . . "

The Great King rode to His Son's side and embraced him before riding back to the Palace at full speed. The guards who had just witnessed this incredible scene offered to go with the Prince, to protect Him from dying sooner than He otherwise might. But the Crown Prince would have none of it and rode off alone.

Indeed it was as He'd been told. Not merely were the peasant folk dressed in black, but a grey pall had settled over every farm and homestead where black clothing hung on clothes lines and where black figures moved about like so many shadowy ghosts over the ground.

* * *

Where it all Starts. . .

> **Isaiah 25:9** And it shall be said in that day, Lo, this *is* our God; we have waited for him, and he will save us: this *is* the LORD; we have waited for him, we will be glad and rejoice in his salvation.

Hit by Lightening!!!

We start off with what so many people seem to ask for when they think of God making Himself known to them.

> **Isaiah 64:1** Oh, that You would rend the heavens! That You would come down! That the mountains might shake at Your presence
>
> **Luke 2:6-7** And so it was, that, while they were there, the days were accomplished that she should be delivered. ⁷And she brought forth her firstborn son, and wrapped him in swaddling clothes, and laid him in a manger; because there was no room for them in the inn.

How often do we pray asking God to show Himself in a major way, ask for mighty displays of His power or expect fire to fall from heaven? And yet. . . His answer is to show up in the little things, in the seemingly powerless things, coming gently and softly.

In the verse above, we see Isaiah pleading that God would show up in great and awesome power! So many people today ask God to show up in great miracles, signs and wonders. God indeed did come down in the most miraculous way possible, as a baby, taking on human form that would one day most definitely rend the very curtain separating the Holy of Holies from the common man! This baby's advent, Jesus Christ, has shaken the mountains of nations, of stubborn hearts, and changed the course of history!

There was another Old Testament personality who would learn this lesson. . .

> **1 Kings 19:1-18** specifically, **1 Kings 19:11-12** And he said, Go forth, and stand upon the mount before the LORD. And, behold, the LORD passed by, and a great and strong wind rent the mountains, and brake in pieces the rocks before the LORD; but the LORD was not in the wind: and after the wind an earthquake; but the LORD was not in the earthquake: ¹²And after the earthquake a fire; but the LORD was not in the fire: and after the fire a still small voice.

With all the awesome power God has to stir up the weather, flood the earth, make the sun stand still, raise up people from the dead and halt whole armies, God still chooses to show His power through gentleness to the human soul. Gentleness has been described much like meekness. . . great power under great control. . . and so it was that God would answer Isaiah's cry with a tiny baby in the manger of a grazing animal. This baby would grow and personify God's meekness and gentleness to all mankind.

What Elijah and Isaiah learned is what God desires for all of us to learn, not just at Christmas when Christianity celebrates Christ's birth, but throughout all our days. The Great God of the Universe desires room in our hearts through the still small voice of His Holy Spirit given room in us through our acceptance of His Word made incarnate in the form of Christ Jesus. I do pray that we truly come to accept the gentle power of God's love presented to us every Christmas; because it doesn't stop there.

Christmas more than any other time of year should bring about such a wave of gratitude, of worship, of humble amazement and thankfulness that the God of the Universe came down as a baby to one day grow up to walk the way of the Cross, die for our sins, rise again to grant eternal life, and seek to touch us so intimately in relationship with us, to call us His eternal Bride, to one day wed us and rule with us for eternity!!!

I find it amazing how this thought ties in so closely with the concept of gentleness as given in the Fruit of the Spirit. That it would cover the very subject of God's sending Christ to earth, that it would show God's awesome power wrapped up in a seemingly helpless package. It takes such willingness to be humbled like that. Instead of just knocking Satan and his hordes to the ends of the universe, instead of marching in and taking us all captive by force to His saving power, God chose to be the gentleman instead of the cosmic bulldozer; Great power under Great control.

Self-control is another Fruit of the Spirit that allowed God to display His love to us through the gentlest means He knew existed. . . that of a soft-skinned, perfectly-formed little baby boy. . . We will see this combination repeat itself over and over and over as we go through these pages together. . .

Love plus self-control equals the rest of the Fruit of the Spirit!

Christmas began this path! How can we not respond with an unhindered show of devotion, praise and worship and fresh submission to His awesome will in our lives?!

That baby in the manger isn't a baby anymore! He is returning soon as our conquering King and glorious Heavenly Bridegroom coming to claim His Bride as His own!

To read Scriptures referenced in this chapter,
please visit http://songdove.fa-ct.com/
There you will find interactive Scripture references, videos containing lyrics to most of the songs in these chapters, topics mentioned in this chapter, and more.

Scriptures used, referred to or that relate to thoughts in this session:

Isaiah 25:9	Luke 2:6-7	1 Kings 19:1-18
Isaiah 64:1		

Topics discussed, referred to, or that relate to thoughts in this session:

Salvation	Power	The Church
Calvary	Love	Bride of Christ

Questions for Discussion:

What comes to mind when you think of the Cross of Calvary?

_____

_____

What do you expect when you think of God making Himself real to you?

_____

_____

What cry was heard in Isaiah and answered in Luke?

Isaiah 64:1_____

Luke 2:6-7_____

Who else would experience this contrast? 1 Kings 19:18

_____

How did God make Himself real in both of these situations?

_____

_____

World's Biggest 2x4!

However at the same time as God presented Himself to us in the gentlest way possible, exhibiting great power under great control to produce the greatest miracle the world would ever know, there comes a time when "Love must be tough". A friend commented that sometimes love carries a 2x4 and that perhaps the biggest 2x4 ever wielded was the Cross Christ died on.

> **John 3:18-21** He that believeth on him is not condemned: but he that believeth not is condemned already, because he hath not believed in the name of the only begotten Son of God. [19]And this is the condemnation, that light is come into the world, and men loved darkness rather than light, because their deeds were evil. [20]For every one that doeth evil hateth the light, neither cometh to the light, lest his deeds should be reproved. [21]But he that doeth truth cometh to the light, that his deeds may be made manifest, that they are wrought in God.

So much of the time we who have accepted Christ as Lord and Saviour are wrapped in awe and wonder, in overflowing wells of gratitude for all that God did in our hearts the moment we came to Christ. Christ offered us an olive branch on the Cross. Our judgement for our sin had already been handed down while we were in our sin, but Christ offered a way out of it by extending the invitation to come to the Cross. We didn't negotiate with God for our salvation. It was either accept, or reject. We accepted and the benefits have been literally amazing!!!

> **Romans 3:23** For all have sinned, and come short of the glory of God;
>
> **Romans 6:23** For the wages of sin *is* death; but the gift of God *is* eternal life through Jesus Christ our Lord.

At the Cross there is no hashing over of past sins, there is no hashing out of how we figure God hurt us and how we hurt God. There is simply repentance, acknowledgement and brokenness over our sin, our wrongdoing, and our wrong thinking and speaking, asking God for forgiveness for these sins, receiving His forgiveness, having our sins washed under the Blood, getting up, placing Christ on the throne of our lives, and allowing the Holy Spirit to guide our actions as we move forward.

Indeed Christ doesn't negotiate with us over our sin. He doesn't let us decide how much of the hurt and blame rests on His shoulders and how much rests on our own. He simply says to accept His gift of forgiveness or reject it. We have no choice but to take full blame for our sins and bring it to Christ and place it at His feet as is, no negotiating of any kind. When we look at it that way, the Cross is a form of tough love. It forces us to say that yes, we were the ones to choose sin, we were the ones born in sin, we were the ones to commit all the wrongs piled on our heads. Because only when we realize our depth of depravity, only when we realize our need for Christ's forgiveness can we truly repent and accept that forgiveness.

Too often people pray the sinner's prayer without that conviction, without the knowledge that they are responsible for their sin, that wrongdoing is sin period! The sinner's prayer is just a life jacket or a parachute pack and a heavy one that most people end up discovering they can't bear on their own. They have failed to truly repent and put Christ on the throne of their lives. They have failed to see the need to turn from their ways and allow the Spirit to guide them into the way of Truth.

> **John 3:16** For God so loved the world, that he gave his only begotten Son, that whosoever believeth in him should not perish, but have everlasting life.

The Cross is a symbol of God's greatest gift to mankind. . . unconditional pardon!!! God loved the world so much that He gave His only Son, that whoever believes in Him would be saved and not perish.

God took the first step toward us by making the way open for forgiveness to be had and He did this in the most amazingly gentle way possible when He sent Christ to earth. But there was no negotiating on God's part with man, that if man cleaned up his act God would come down. There was no negotiating on man's part with God, that if God owned up to the pain He was inflicting on the world that man would come to the Cross. There is no room for negotiation at the Cross. There is only room for repentance. Only then does the Blood wash us clean, only then does Christ impart to us that beautiful Robe of Righteousness, only then do we become joint heirs with Christ and members of the Bride of Christ, the Church.

God longs for all of mankind to accept His offer. God set down the conditions of acceptance, all we must do is humble ourselves, admit our sin, seek forgiveness and it is offered to us the moment we do so. God doesn't hold back, can't hold back! He so deeply longs for us to come to Him, to wrap His arms around us, to rescue us from the judgement we've meted out for ourselves, to restore us to Himself.

The old rugged Cross. . . that symbol of triumph over Satan and sin. . . symbol of forgiveness. . . symbol of an incredibly infinite love by an eternal holy God. . .

The best part is. . . it's empty!!! Christ rose from the dead to grant us eternal life with Him forever!!! We couldn't negotiate a better deal if we tried!!!

To view lyrics for songs referenced in this chapter,
please visit http://songdove.fa-ct.com/
There you will find interactive Scripture references, videos containing lyrics to most of the songs listed here, topics mentioned in this chapter, and more.

Scriptures used, referred to or that relate to thoughts in this session:

Romans 3:23	Romans 5:8	John 3:16
Romans 3:10-18	Romans 10:9	
Romans 6:23	Romans 10:13	

Songs shared, referenced, or that relate to thoughts in this session:

The Old Rugged Cross

Topics discussed, referred to, or that relate to thoughts in this session:

Salvation   Power   Love
Calvary

Questions for Discussion:

What comes to mind when you think of the concept of love being tough?

_____

_____

What does coming to the Cross mean to you?

_____

_____

Can we negotiate with God? Explain. . .

_____

_____

Who carries the blame for mankind's sinful nature?

_____

The Old Rugged Cross

Chorus 1

So I'll cherish the old rugged cross, Till my trophies at last I lay down

I will cling to the old rugged cross, And exchange it some day for a crown

Verse 1

On a hill far away, Stood an old rugged cross

The emblem of suff'ring and shame, And I love that old cross

Where the dearest and best, For a world of lost sinners was slain

Verse 2

Oh the old rugged cross, So despised by the world

Has a wondrous attraction for me, For the dear Lamb of God

Left His glory above, To bear it to dark Calvary

Verse 3

In the old rugged cross, Stained with blood so divine

A wondrous beauty I see, For 'twas on that old cross

Jesus suffered and died, To pardon and sanctify me

Verse 4

To the old rugged cross, I will ever be true

Its shame and reproach gladly bear, Then He'll call me some day

To my home far away ,Where His glory forever I'll share

CCLI Song No. 19722
© Public Domain
George Bennard

Free-will or Predestination, this author's interpretation:

> **Rom 3:23** For all have sinned, and come short of the glory of God;

> **John 3:14-17** And as Moses lifted up the serpent in the wilderness, even so must the Son of man be lifted up: [15]That whosoever believeth in him should not perish, but have eternal life. [16]For God so loved the world, that he gave his only begotten Son, that whosoever believeth in him should not perish, but have everlasting life. [17]For God sent not his Son into the world to condemn the world; but that the world through him might be saved.

Some people try to say that God already knows and has picked out ahead of time, chosen the way one chooses a car or picks out linens for the bridal suite, those who are destined to be with Him in heaven one day. Others teach that ALL are welcome into God's Kingdom and that God is aware of all who will make that decision to come to Him. In light of eternity, what matters is that we follow the pattern of Salvation given by Christ and confirmed by Paul and others. Too many verses show God truly IS concerned for ALL mankind, not desiring that ANY should perish.

There are those for whom it's not worth my emotional and physical health to get them to see this when they are firmly set against it. They can explain away every single verse you give them. All doesn't mean ALL, any doesn't mean ANY. "Elect" means "to the exclusion of anyone else who may desire to come to Christ", and the goats were people who "got saved and Christ said He never knew them", totally missing the reason Christ said He never knew them, not the saved part at all, but the doing part, their fruit did not show evidence of Salvation at all, they were paying lip service, they had not served God with all their mind, soul, heart and strength.

"Whosoever will may come", God calls them His elect. I'd liken God's fore-knowledge to someone watching a tomatoe plant produce early fruit, and how the observer notices that a few will be bigger and rounder than the others, and chooses to call them their best tomatoes before they are even ripe. This is the only way to reconcile God's foreknowledge with His desire that ALL mankind be saved, that no one perish in their sins, and His sadness and grief over those that turn their backs on His offer of Salvation. Why would God grieve over those He deliberately turns away? I don't see that anywhere in Scripture. Mankind's continual refusal eventually moves God to anger, to the Day of Wrath we call the Tribulation. If He didn't care, He wouldn't even get angry. My God invited all to come to Him, He sent Christ to die for the sins of ALL mankind, not just a select few.

To read Scriptures referenced in this chapter,
please visit http://songdove.fa-ct.com/
There you will find interactive Scripture references, videos containing lyrics to most of the songs in these chapters, topics mentioned in this chapter, and more.

Scriptures used, referred to or that relate to thoughts in this session:

John 3: 13-21	1 Peter 1:2	Matthew 24:22
Romans 5:1	Isaiah 42:1-13	Matthew 25:32-46

Topics discussed, referred to, or that relate to thoughts in this session:

Salvation	Power	Love
Calvary		

Questions for Discussion:

When God says He would that ALL would be saved in John 3:16, do you think He means ALL? Why or why not?

_____

_____

Who are the Elect in the Old and New Testament?

_____

_____

Who are the sheep and goats in Christ's parable in Matthew 25:32-46?

_____

_____

Use the topical search tool the website to study terms related to faith, works, salvation, etc. Write your findings below:

_____

_____

_____

_____

_____

_____

The Bridal Call:

Everywhere I turn these days, it seems as if I'm running into Christians who are talking about the need to go deeper in their worship, calling it a sacred romance. I think I've heard that term now at least 4 different times since mid-2007. The latest time was from Alvin Slaughter as he told his story of how he'd become disillusioned with church and of how God was wooing him back. He called intimate worship a "sacred romance".

That desire to touch heart to heart, Spirit to spirit, mind to mind seems to be awakening in so many people both on the Internet and on the street. Others have said that what they see in Christian conferences and rallies is great, but that it needs to be not just a weekend thing, but real and alive right here in our own churches and in our own lives. What we experience in a worship concert wasn't meant to be a one-time thing, but a daily lived out experience! This observation came from a guy who broke out into prayer during a half-hour of worship after choir one night, who was so overwhelmed with the corporate yet individual hug God gave all of us, that he could barely find words to describe the love he felt God lavishing over everyone!!!

Some have referred this awakening, this reviving of hearts, as God awakening His Bride, calling forth the Bridal heart of His Church. If this is the case, its happening all over the world! It appears too that those of us on western shores may be late to the table, but alongside myself, others are coming. Others are becoming more and more desirous to have that intimate meeting with God in their times of worship. The awesome thing about it is that God is so quick to show up and meet this desire in not just my life, but in others' lives as well. God just can't stay away from anyone who shows a desire to get in deeper with Him, as if God has been love-starved and now that His prize creation is waking up to the fact He longs to love us in ways we never dreamed were more than just words on the pages of Scripture, He can't resist it and shows up every chance someone opens up to Him.

Tying it all Together:

> **Ephesians 5:25-27** Husbands, love your wives, even as Christ also loved the church, and gave himself for it; [26]That he might sanctify and cleanse it with the washing of water by the word, [27]That he might present it to himself a glorious church, not having spot, or wrinkle, or any such thing; but that it should be holy and without blemish.

So we have God's great power and might wrapped up in a baby in the manger who would grow to walk the way to the Cross, offering us a non-negotiable offer of unconditional pardon and life everlasting in His Kingdom if we would admit our sin, turn from it, and seek Him with all our hearts! This Christ, this Jesus of Nazareth, rose from the dead to grant all who would come to Him eternal life forever, kinship as sons, as children of God, but more than kinship, He has called us His Bride. The Church around the world has been referred to in the pages of Scripture as the Bride of Christ!

So our journey toward living as that Bride of Christ, toward preparing ourselves for our eternal Bridegroom, starts at the foot of the Cross. It is there where we first experience the deep desperation that drove Christ to die for the Bride He longs to bring to His side! It is there we discover just how passionate His love is for us, that He would die for us even when we were not worthy to set foot in His Throne room! It is at the foot of the Cross where we lay our sins at His feet, humble ourselves before Him, admit our wretched condition, and accept His beautiful robe of righteousness in return! That robe that allows God the Father to look on us, call us His Children, and present us to His Son as that radiant Bride that we will learn in the coming pages how to become.

Isaiah 61:10-11 I will greatly rejoice in the LORD, my soul shall be joyful in my God; for he hath clothed me with the garments of salvation, he hath covered me with the robe of righteousness, as a bridegroom decketh himself with ornaments, and as a bride adorneth herself with her jewels. [11]For as the earth bringeth forth her bud, and as the garden causeth the things that are sown in it to spring forth; so the Lord GOD will cause righteousness and praise to spring forth before all the nations.

This is a journey God began to place me on in the spring of 2007. It is a journey that has been fraught with challenges, with coming face to face with impurities and having to deal with them, of some of the most intimate moments I have ever had with my Lord and Saviour as He teaches me how to live with Him as unseen Husband in this home.

If you read this opening chapter, and made a decision for Christ for the very first time, what follows should be taken slowly, and with a mentor who can help you understand as you go.

If you read this chapter and you've been saved for some time, this may be your opportunity to discover a deeper relationship than what you have known to date. Share it with someone. Go into the Scriptures that will be shared and ask God to prepare you for your part, for your role in the Bride of Christ.

We have come to the Cross and bowed to its demands, we have been washed clean of our sin and given the Robe of Righteousness. Now it is time to prepare ourselves for our wedding day!

Step into my heart and mind now, as I begin to unveil the heart of this worshipper. . .

To read Scriptures referenced in this chapter,
please visit http://songdove.fa-ct.com/
There you will find interactive Scripture references, videos containing lyrics to
most of the songs in these chapters, topics mentioned in this chapter, and
more.

Scriptures used, referred to or that relate to thoughts in this session:

Isaiah 61:10-11   Ephesians 5:25-27

Topics discussed, referred to, or that relate to thoughts in this session:

Salvation   Love   Righteousness
Calvary   Bride
Power   Church

Questions for Discussion:

Have you been given the Robe of Righteousness? Why or why not?

_____

_____

What will you do with what you have read? _____

_____

In a Land, Far, Far away. . . But Closer than Any of Us Realize. . . the Following Story Continued. . .

Years passed, the Crown Prince was back on His throne by His Father's side. The great hall was filled as before, but those in black had been banished and were no longer welcome among the busy throngs. Outside palace walls and beyond the Capital City, the Realm was now a patchwork quilt of white and black, and even grey as groups of peasantry tried to live in both the white and black ways.

The Crown Prince would saddle up Swift Wind more often now to ride the paths and trails that wound among the hamlets and farms. Those in black would hide as He approached, busying themselves with tasks away from His piercing eyes. Those in grey would meet Him in the way, giving elaborate excuses for trying to live not just for the Great King, but for the Black Guard as well. The Crown Prince would move on in sorrow, shaking His head as He went. Those dressed in white would see Him coming and invite Him into their humble homes. They would celebrate with singing and dance. . . or at least they used to.

Times had changed. The white robes were now more important than the One who had supplied them. Looking after those robes became higher priority than spending time with the Crown Prince or the Great King! Father and Son pled with the people to come to them, to join them in the Great Hall, that arms were always open if they would but humble themselves and show gratitude for the sacrifice the Crown Prince had made for them. A new form of black had begun to creep in among those dressed in white. It was still white, but only white on the outside. This garment had to be put on carefully so that the black underside did not show, and the Crown Prince could see it. . .

One day as He rode through the countryside, He observed a commotion in the distance. A young lady dressed in white was being attacked by men in grey and black. One of the men in grey was trying to encourage the girl to put on grey so the attack would cease, but she wouldn't do it. She'd known in her heart it was wrong to court a man in grey, but she'd done it anyway and knew that she was paying the price for her poor judgement. Soon she was left lying in the ditch, her white garments torn and covered in blood and dirt.

She lay there, ashamed to get up, knowing that if she did so and was seen by her fellow countrymen, that she'd be banished from her village and forced to live alone. There was nowhere for her to go.

The Crown Prince had observed this from miles away and it would be many days before He would reach her region of the Realm. The young lady did what she could to clean herself up, trying to reintegrate with her townsfolk. Those who did not know of her past did not question, although eyebrows would be raised occasionally whenever a scar or a rip was revealed. The girl felt every stare acutely, and as much as she tried to fit back in, she still felt alone and hurting.

One day as she was out walking by the side of the very same road where she'd been attacked, she looked up and saw the most amazing sight! A man dressed in white was riding a white horse. White horses were unheard of in her part of the Realm for starters. But the man on the horse was no ordinary peasant! His clothing shone like the sun and glint of the metal clasps on the horse's bridle nearly blinded her. As He rode up, the gentleness of His gaze nearly had her run for cover behind a nearby bush, but her legs wouldn't carry her and she collapsed to the ground.

The Crown Prince dismounted his steed, admonishing Swift Wind to stay nearby. Swift Wind nickered softly as he found a patch of grass to nibble. The Prince walked over to the young lady and knelt beside her. Expecting judgement and berating, the girl hid her face in her hair, refusing to look up. Gently and tenderly, the Prince placed a finger under her chin and lifted her eyes to His. The girl's countenance turned from fear to amazement as she saw the most amazing love radiate from His face. The Prince brushed her hair from her face, revealing a festering wound on her cheek. She winced as a strand was removed. When the Prince moved to touch the wound, she re-coiled, trying to pull away. But the Prince held her close, whispering in her ear, "Many daughters have done virtuously, but you excel them all."

She couldn't help blushing at those words, relaxing a little in spite of herself, but feeling incredible shame at having been found in such a state by one so amazingly gentle and kind. She did not yet know she was in the hands of the Crown Prince over all the Realm.

Ever so tenderly, the Crown Prince persuaded her to let Him touch the wound on her cheek. As soon as she allowed Him, the wound healed, leaving only a faint mark where it once was. The girl touched her cheek in astonishment! Who was this man?!

As the Crown Prince gazed into the beauty of the young lady's face, He knew deep within His heart. . . He had found His Bride!

* * *

The Prince of Peace Rides In. . .

> **Psalm 100:1-5** A Psalm of praise. Make a joyful noise unto the LORD, all ye lands. ²Serve the LORD with gladness: come before his presence with singing. ³Know ye that the LORD he *is* God: *it is* he *that* hath made us, and not we ourselves; *we are* his people, and the sheep of his pasture. ⁴Enter into his gates with thanksgiving, *and* into his courts with praise: be thankful unto him, *and* bless his name. ⁵For the LORD *is* good; his mercy *is* everlasting; and his truth *endureth* to all generations.

> **Colossians 1:19-20** For it pleased *the Father* that in him should all fulness dwell; ²⁰And, having made peace through the blood of his cross, by him to reconcile all things unto himself; by him, *I say,* whether *they be* things in earth, or things in heaven.

In our Unworthy State

"When He Was on The Cross, I Was on His Mind" How amazing it is that a peasant girl like me would be the recipient of the intimate love of her King. That He would step from the courts of Heaven and seek me among the hovels of earth, take me in His arms and pledge His love to me. But that's exactly what God did. He did look down from heaven. He saw what had happened in the Garden of Eden, and set in motion the greatest rescue mission ever to take place!

How unworthy I feel when I think of this thought, how amazed, yet how grateful too as I look back and see how He's provided for so many needs particularly during my life as a single parent. That He would lavish so much love on someone like me, who if it weren't for the stranglehold on my faith that keeps me going, would have destroyed my life by looking for love, acceptance, protection and security in all the wrong places. There are times I can so solidly identify with Paul when he says in **Romans 7:18** "For I know that in me (that is, in my flesh,) dwelleth no good thing: for to will is present with me; but how to perform that which is good I find not." But then maybe that's why He did seek to overshadow me in this way, and why He has over-shadowed me so intensely since the beginning of March 07. I don't need to look anywhere else. He wants me to look only to Himself. Human as I am, thoughts still sometimes stray, but rather than slap me back to my senses, He waits for me to return my focus to Him again, reminding me of the dangers inherent in even thinking of looking for love in other places. This produces a desire to reset my focus as often and as quickly as I can so that desires for human intimacy don't steal from what God is offering me instead. People will come and go sad to say, but God will always be here, the only real constant in a world that keeps changing whether or not I want it to.

> **Hebrews 10:8-9** Above when he said, Sacrifice and offering and burnt offerings and offering for sin thou wouldest not, neither hadst pleasure therein; which are offered by the law; ⁹Then said he, Lo, I come to do thy will, O God. He taketh away the first, that he may establish the second.

Sometimes people get the impression that they have to earn God's favour. That it is through their own effort and sacrifice that they can enter into that Most Holy Place. I went to visit a friend one time, and he could sense God's overshadowing as soon as I walked in the door. Through the course of conversation, he ended up showing me the above passage. This is part of a larger passage where God explains how He's followed up the law with a better covenant. In those verses God confirmed for me that He is not interested in sacrifices as much as what He sees in our heart. It isn't through anything I could, couldn't, did or didn't do to earn His love for me. What an awesome God we serve!

To view lyrics for songs referenced in this chapter,
please visit http://songdove.fa-ct.com/
There you will find interactive Scripture references, videos containing lyrics to most of the songs listed here, topics mentioned in this chapter, and more.

Scriptures shared, referenced, or that relate to thoughts in this session:

Psalm 100:1-5   Romans 7:14-25   Hebrews 10:1-10
Colossians 1:19

Songs shared, referenced, or that relate to thoughts in this session:

When He Was on The Cross

Topics discussed, referred to, or that relate to thoughts in this session:

Relationship with God and mankind   Refocus
God's strength   God's goodness and kindness

Questions for Discussion:

Spend some time reading Romans Chapters 7 and 8.

What is the focus of chapter 7?_____

What is the focus of Chapter 8?_____

Sometimes our feelings of unworthiness come from past failures. What did
Christ do on the cross for us?

_____

What feelings contribute to unworthiness? _____

_____

How has God made His unconditional love real to you? _____

_____

When He Was On The Cross

CCLI Song No. 104091
© 1984 Wind In Willow Publishing Company | Songs Of Calvary Music (Admin. by Integrated Copyright Group, Inc.) |
Mike Payne | Ronnie Hinson

Man Looks on the Outward Appearance. . .

Praise1065.com, a Christian radio station in the northwest of the USA, around 9pm at night used to switch to a musical format called Sharing Life Together where a female announcer took calls and allowed for the asking of questions and offering of advice, sometimes from herself other times from other callers. One night a guy called in wondering if it was wrong to ask God for an extremely beautiful wife. He was referring to physical beauty. That brought back my own heart's cry to be loved for who I am, not for what I look like. I decided to write in and tell the announcer how I felt about this is - sue. However, God has since shown me that He's really the only One who can truly love me the way I want to be loved. He's really the only One who can love me for who I am instead of for what I look like. He doesn't treat me like a trophy, or wish others could see who He's with. He sees my heart. He sees my head. He even sees the secret parts of me that would turn others off completely and yet still loves me so incredibly, so unconditionally.

> **Proverbs 31:30** Favour is deceitful, and beauty is vain: but a woman that feareth the LORD, she shall be praised.

My personal challenge is to be the woman of **Proverbs 31**, as futile as that seems at times, but then the above verse comes to mind. I am choosing to focus my attention on entering into the depths of the love God has displayed for me, and its life-changing results. God is my Lover, and the only One who is capable of loving me in the manner I have so desperately desired. I thank Him for this whenever the thought comes to mind.

> **1 Samuel 16:7** . . .for the LORD seeth not as man seeth; for man looketh on the outward appearance, but the LORD looketh on the heart.

This reminder has allowed me to be more free in His presence, a freedom I have not felt in a long time. While God cares that I look after the features He's given me, He doesn't base His love for me on that appearance, instead He sees what's on the inside, the real me. This tent will develop wrinkles, sag, lose its shape, and eventually break down. But God will love me no matter what happens to my exterior. I wish I could say this to that guy who called in that one night, but the best I could do was email the announcer. I want to be loved for me, not for what I look like. God has met this heart's cry, and I don't want to leave this revelation.

To read Scriptures referenced in this chapter,
please visit http://songdove.fa-ct.com/
There you will find interactive Scripture references, videos containing lyrics to most of the songs in these chapters, topics mentioned in this chapter, and more.

Scriptures used, referred to or that relate to thoughts in this session:

Proverbs 31   1 Samuel 16:7   Song of Solomon 1:5

Topics discussed, referred to, or that relate to thoughts in this session:

Visual versus Spiritual attractiveness

Questions for Discussion:

In the workbook that accompanied Brian Simmons' book: "Song of Solomon: Journey of the Bride" The following question was asked:

Who is speaking each of these phrases in Song of Solomon 1:5? The Shulamite, or the King?

I am black, _____

But comely, O ye daughters of Jerusalem _____

As the tents of Kedar _____

As the curtains of Solomon. _____

Some of us feel like the Shulamite when looking at our hearts, at our lives, but others of us feel this way when looking at our outward appearance.

Look at Psalm 139, Proverbs 31, and 1 Samuel 16:7 What can we learn from these verses?

_____

_____

_____

The Deeper We Go, the Less Worthy We Feel – Alabaster Box

In May of 2007, Priscilla, a lady from Belfast, Ireland, came to a conference in my town, and told a version of an incident recounted in **Matthew 26, Mark 14 and Luke 7**, of the prostitute who broke an alabaster box over Jesus' feet that had me identify in a way I never anticipated. It was as if I could identify somehow. While I was never a prostitute, while I lived a clean life for the most part short of mistakes that nearly cost my virginity to the man I was engaged to marry and later divorce, I could identify with her on an emotional self-worth level. I began to cry in my heart and when I first recounted this story to others, real tears threatened to fall.

There are times when I still feel so completely unworthy of all that God's done for me, and the more I sense His intimate lover's heart for me personally, the less I feel worthy to receive it and the more in awe I am that He would lavish such love upon someone like me. My story pales in comparison to many single parents who have come through the doors of my church. It's the unseen things where I bear the scars, the unseen things that still come back to haunt and hurt occasionally and that give rise to taunts of unworthiness. Social, emotional, and relational scars and wounds don't show up as broken bones, black bruises or missing patches of hair. They don't show up as health issues caused by alcohol or drugs, but at times I have wondered how long it will take to heal from them.

God has brought me so far since I left my ex. He's restored to me avenues of ministry I thought were long gone, that I'd never be fit for after my divorce. He's taught me various levels of trust, one lesson ending in such an intimate, intensely personal display of God's love I'd never experienced before. But that was one thing Marie, also from Belfast, Ireland, spoke about at this conference in May of 2007. . . she too had felt that she knew God's love, that she loved God, but it was on the service level, it was the love of His hand that she knew, not the love of His heart. Like myself, when God showed her the love of His heart it blew her away. Like another lady I knew, she found herself being taken to **Song of Solomon**, and she showed everyone a verse speaking about how when we lift our eyes to Him, we ravish His heart, that He looks at us and as Marie put it, His heart skips a beat like ours does when someone captivates us.

> **Song of Solomon 4:9** Thou hast ravished my heart, my sister, my spouse; thou hast ravished my heart with one of thine eyes, with one chain of thy neck.

So I bring my alabaster box to the Lord. I weep at His feet, whether in my heart, or in real wet tears falling down my face. I bow my heart before Him and allow it to be broken under the gentle gaze of His loving eyes. I am unworthy to be called His Bride. I am unworthy to be brought into His chamber. I am ashamed of my naked heart and the bruises and scars human eyes cannot see. But I lift my hands and my voice in gratitude and thankfulness. I lift my voice in amazement and wonder that He calls me His own and sees fit to use me in His Kingdom in spite of how I view myself. Once again I am filled with thankfulness and gratefulness that God sees me through the righteousness of Christ. Christ has removed the rags of sin, did that in my life way back at the age of 7 when I accepted Him as Saviour and Lord, and has put on me the robe of His own righteousness. If it weren't for the robe of righteousness that only Christ can give, I truly would be unworthy, not merely feeling as if I am.

> **Isaiah 61:10** I will greatly rejoice in the LORD, my soul shall be joyful in my God; for he hath clothed me with the garments of salvation, he hath covered me with the robe of righteousness, as a bridegroom decketh himself with ornaments, and as a bride adorneth herself with her jewels.

We have such an awesome God, such unconditional love no matter how we view ourselves or how we handle life and the tasks He's given us to accomplish. "I'll Take You Back" is a song that rings so true for me. Music imparts such a powerful message, especially anointed music inspired by the Holy Spirit and hearts full of gratitude toward Him. That is when I feel closest to my Lord and it seems God meets me so. . . nearly tangibly. . . I love this time when it comes.

To view lyrics for songs referenced in this chapter,
please visit http://songdove.fa-ct.com/
There you will find interactive Scripture references, videos containing lyrics to
most of the songs listed here, topics mentioned in this chapter, and more.

Scriptures used, referred to or that relate to thoughts in this session:

Matthew 26	Luke 7	Isaiah 61:10
Mark 14	Song of Songs 4:9	

Songs shared, referenced, or that relate to thoughts in this session:

Take You Back

Topics discussed, referred to, or that relate to thoughts in this session:

Alabaster box	Self-forgiveness versus God's forgive-
Lessons in trust	ness
Refocus	God's goodness and kindness

Questions for Discussion:

What happens to our view of ourselves, the closer we get to Christ? _____

_____

Sometimes our feelings of unworthiness come from past failures. What did
Christ do on the cross for us?

_____

_____

What feelings contribute to unworthiness? _____

_____

Too many of us know the love of God's _____ rather than the
love of His _____.

How Can I Keep From Singing

CCLI Song No. 4822372

© 2006 worshiptogether.com songs | sixsteps Music | Alletrop Music | Thankyou Music | Vamos Publishing (Admin. by EMI Christian Music Publishing) | (Admin. by EMI Christian Music Publishing) | (Admin. by Music Services, Inc.) | (Admin. by EMI Christian Music Publishing) | (Admin. by EMI Christian Music Publishing)

Chris Tomlin | Ed Cash | Matt Redman

Take You Back

CCLI Song No. 4504250

© 2004 Thirsty Moon River Publishing | Stolen Pride (Admin. by EMI Christian Music Publishing) | (Admin. by EMI Christian Music Publishing)

Jeremy Camp

Jesus Friend Of Sinners

CCLI Song No. 2573623

© 1998 Thankyou Music (Admin. by EMI Christian Music Publishing)

Paul Oakley

The Deeper We Go, the Less Worthy We Feel – Self Acceptance

The whole bit about being accepted by God in spite of my weaknesses, my failings, and my mistakes keeps hitting me afresh. I don't understand everything He is doing in my life. Why He chooses to do things at certain times occasionally leaves me clueless, I am currently clueless as to His timing now regarding dealing with my scars and wounds that relate to how He made me. I got the distinct message one morning that I needed to lay that at the foot of the Cross. . . I have issues with singing songs that cannot be made real in my life and we'd sung a song that morning called "At The Foot of the Cross", by Kathryn Scott.

Every worship song is either something I mean wholeheartedly toward God or His people, something I wish to make real in my own life, or something God is trying to speak to me about, and that morning's song choices were no different. I found myself singing "Jesus, Friend of Sinners" by Paul Oakley, in a very personal way.

As one of the songs on Praise106.5 says, "how can I keep from singing Your praise, how can I ever say enough, 'how amazing is Your love', How can I keep from shouting Your praise, I am loved by the King, and it makes my heart want to sing".

I have felt God's gentle comforting touch so closely at times during worship sets that I felt the occasional tear threaten to well up. Ashes into beauty, a peace that calms our fears. . . A God who takes pleasure in what He made, seeking to restore it, restore me, to the intention and appearance first desired.

It's my prayerful desire that you my reader, step further into God's invitation to deeper intimacy with Him. God doesn't cut corners. As I have walked this road, there has been pain as God has dealt with issues needing His healing, restoring touch. There will be pain for you too, as stuff gets dredged up to be removed and healed, as much I'm sure you are hoping you can skip the dredging part and just move to the healing part.

To view lyrics for songs referenced in this chapter,
please visit http://songdove.fa-ct.com/
There you will find interactive Scripture references, videos containing lyrics to
most of the songs listed here, topics mentioned in this chapter, and more.

Songs shared, referenced, or that relate to thoughts in this session:

At the Foot of the Cross   How Can I Keep From Singing
Jesus, Friend of Sinners

Topics discussed, referred to, or that relate to thoughts in this session:

Self-acceptance   God's goodness and kindness
Worship

Questions for Discussion:

When and in what circumstances do you feel closest to God? Musical expression, acts of service, private times in the Word, moments of prayer, write them here:

_____

_____

How does deliberate engagement in lyrical worship serve as a catalyst to focus our attention on God?

_____

_____

Maybe you are one of those people who enter into worship in a non-lyrical way. What ways do you enter into worship and how does that help to refocus your attention on God?

_____

_____

How Can I Keep From Singing

CCLI Song No. 4822372

© 2006 worshiptogether.com songs | sixsteps Music | Alletrop Music | Thankyou Music | Vamos Publishing (Admin. by EMI Christian Music Publishing) | (Admin. by EMI Christian Music Publishing) | (Admin. by Music Services, Inc.) | (Admin. by EMI Christian Music Publishing) | (Admin. by EMI Christian Music Publishing)

Chris Tomlin | Ed Cash | Matt Redman

Take You Back

CCLI Song No. 4504250

© 2004 Thirsty Moon River Publishing | Stolen Pride (Admin. by EMI Christian Music Publishing) | (Admin. by EMI Christian Music Publishing)

Jeremy Camp

Jesus Friend Of Sinners

CCLI Song No. 2573623

© 1998 Thankyou Music (Admin. by EMI Christian Music Publishing)

Paul Oakley

At The Foot Of The Cross

CCLI Song No. 4157353

© 2003 Vertical Worship Songs (Admin. by EMI Christian Music Publishing)

Kathryn Scott

Surrendering My Shame

Shame. . . it hits in various ways at various times, invariably caused by knowledge of what's true and right contrasted to some thought, word or behaviour that was contrary to that knowledge. I will share a few thoughts at this time, from my own experiences.

Knowledge versus Action

As I've gone through life as a Christian from age 7 onward, and since beginning this journey into God's heart back in 2007, I can honestly say that there are times when it's tempting to let the shame of what I should know versus what I've gone through take over. Perhaps it's just me not fully allowing myself to surrender to this obvious reshaping of my head and heart in God's hands. Other times it's "fear of man" versus having fallen from the high bar I'd once set for myself and wondering if I'll ever reach that expectation again. Regardless of the reasons, I am starting to get the nudge to bow myself before the Lord in surrender and gratitude any time I sense shame, to trade my shame for surrender to the One who accepts me no matter what I've done, thought, felt, or been through. I know where this came from, and once again it returns to the place God has lovingly held me captive, the lyrics of some of the songs we sing, about how God has removed our shame, about trading our sorrows. . . "Trading My Sorrows (Yes Lord)" . . . by Darrell Evans:

I don't know how many times I've sung that song, but I now see the practical application of it. Trade my shame for His acceptance. . . Seems I can momentarily let go of my shame when I am in the intimate presence of my God. But that song "Trading My Sorrows" speaks more of where I'd like to be than where I am half the time. It's one of those songs where I sing them desiring them to be true of my life rather than stating that I've arrived. I want to trade my shame for the Joy of the Lord. At some point there must be a place where I've given it up, let go of it, and only the enemy tries to bring it back to haunt me.

How many, like myself can say that I've repeatedly asked God for forgiveness in my choices. . . thinking that by now He's probably asking me what I'm talking about, He forgave and forgot when I asked the first time. Part of it is being able to forgive myself and that can be a struggle. I still beat myself up over my part in my life's black blot (the divorce I went through back in '99-'01).

It's because I had a part to play that its so amazing to find myself doing so much in God's House once again and why it's so hard sometimes to believe I'm actually qualified in God's eyes to be doing what I'm doing. Talk about humbling! If I were in charge of what I were given to do, I'd probably still be hiding in the third row of the choir, not doing much of anything. But praise the Lord He's the One in control. "Cry Out to Jesus" by Third Day is another one with the message of mercy and healing. This one has touched me so often.

Shame before God over wrongdoing is one thing, and should lead one to healing and forgiveness as stated in the last paragraph. Then there is shame before others because of status or fear of man as in this next illustration brought out as I looked at Psalm 81.

Psalm 81

> **Psalm 81:13** Oh that my people had hearkened unto me, and Israel had walked in my ways!

From verses 5 to the end of the psalm, God reminisces of all that He did to draw the people of Israel out of Egypt, how He cared for them and provided for them. But God laments that they turned their hearts from Him, they would not listen to Him. . . pleading in verse 13 above that His people had walked in His ways. God goes on to say that He would have come to their defence, He would have struck their adversaries. But God was prevented from doing this by their hatred toward Him, and by their refusal to submit to Him. . . Do you see that? We prevent God from coming to our rescue as He would like, when we refuse to submit to Him. I can personally testify to this truth in my own life, particularly as it has come to finances. God had to drill out of me what my parents had drilled into me, that I had to be self-sufficient and provide for myself! I was taught not to rely on others, or to expect others to help me out. It took God several years before I would get the lesson that I was to surrender my pride, submit myself to God's provision no matter how He thought to give it, and learn to humble myself and ask for help. Let me tell you I have vowed never to repeat those lessons again! It is humbling every time I have to rely on others for provision.

The way some people do things, it can leave me feeling shame that I am unable to afford what most others around me can. To avoid those feelings of shame in the past, I simply didn't open my mouth or show up where funds were needed. God brought people along who have seen through my silence, seen the reason for that silence, and who have determined that missing out due to lack of affordability will end as long as they have anything to do with it! It's different to say the least. I'm not used to that. I tell these people occasionally that I don't want to take advantage of them, because that is the other reason for shame, when others feel you are freeloading instead of acting on legitimate offers of help.

But the lessons leading up to these developments were very hard indeed. God had to break my financial independent streak. Once I finally got the message, I wasted no time in submitting to God's hand and heart toward me, and an adventure began that has been exciting, frustrating, amazing, hair-pulling, and increasingly intimate toward my God as I have learned to submit in more areas than just my finances.

Verse 16 bites at the end of this psalm. . . speaking of those who refused to turn to Him, God says, "He should have fed them also with the finest of the wheat: and with honey out of the rock should I have satisfied thee." Oh the blessings we forfeit when we refuse to bow our hearts before our Creator, our King, our Heavenly Father, and the Lover of our souls. . . These blessings are not necessarily financial. Many of them are quite decidedly otherwise. But the riches found through whole-hearted surrender to God, are too many to tell. Financially I have had to admit that we are poor. Not on the streets, but among the working poor as the classification has been coined. However in pretty much every other way I can think of, God has blessed us, surprised us, spoiled us, and shared in those blessings with us as unseen Husband and Father in this home.

This subject will continue with tomorrow's reading.

To view lyrics for songs referenced in this chapter,
please visit http://songdove.fa-ct.com/

There you will find interactive Scripture references, videos containing lyrics to most of the songs listed here, topics mentioned in this chapter, and more.

Scriptures used, referred to or that relate to thoughts in this session:

Psalm 81

Songs shared, referenced, or that relate to thoughts in this session:

Trading My Sorrows   Cry Out to Jesus

Topics discussed, referred to, or that relate to thoughts in this session:

Failure	Chastisement
Shame	Trust
Surrender	Finances
Forgiveness	Fear of man
Humility	

Questions for Discussion:

Has your knowledge versus your actions ever caused you shame? Explain. . .

_____

_____

_____

Who accepts you no matter how deep your shame feels?

_____

_____

Go to this book's companion website, Click on Chapter 2, and watch the lyrics of "Cry Out to Jesus" by Third Day. Have you ever been in situations spoken of in this song? Care to share?

_____

_____

_____

When is shame actually a sign of refusal to surrender?

_____

_____

Surrendering My Shame Part 2

The Psalmist felt shame before others in another Psalm too. As I read through Psalm 44, it became clear to me that in the Psalmist's experience, his shame had been used as a tool to humble him. I don't know about my reader, but I had never thought of shame as a tool toward humility before. Allow me to share this particular study as well:

Psalm 44

Being steadfast in faith, obedience and focus even in the face of chastening, difficulty, and hard times that we don't always make sense of is a quality God looks for in His people. . .

The Psalmist knew this as he penned this psalm, recounting tales of God's protection, deliverance and provision, stating that he will not trust his own sword to save him but place that trust in God Himself. The Psalmist was a Warrior-Shepherd King let us not forget. But he knew that ultimate victory could never come in exploits of battle. Only the God of Israel could bring true victory, true deliverance.

This recounting of God's exploits on behalf of the people of Israel is necessary in order for the next part of this psalm to make sense. The Psalmist speaks of feeling cast aside, made into a derision among his enemies, of defeat before them. But he doesn't wallow in those feelings. Instead he turns his face toward God and says that no matter how bad things get, he will still trust God, will still serve God, has not turned aside in his faith to other gods, and challenges God to prove that this is true within his heart. Reminds me of Job when he said,

> **Job 13:15** Though he slay me, yet will I trust in him: but I will maintain mine own ways before him.

It is important to remember that chastening never feels good at the time. Sometimes it really does feel as if God has turned His face away from us for a season. But the truth is that God is carrying out this discipline to shape us, mold us, cleanse us and humble us as in the outcome of this particular psalm, and to make us into the people He originally intended for us to be.

The Psalmist chooses the path that pleases God by choosing to be humble before Him. The Psalmist goes so far as to say that the circumstances God has allowed in his life, have humbled him. How many of us would say the same thing if we were honest with ourselves? That the circumstances God has allowed have humbled us? I know I have to say that. I can point to time after time when God has had to humble me for various reasons, to remind me that I am completely and totally dependent upon Him and not anything I can say or do of myself. I have written extensively about this in times past, how I have come to realize that in and of myself, I can do no good thing, that I am reliant, dependent, deeply in need of the Holy Spirit living through me to the world around me.

> **Psalm 44:4-5** Thou art my King, O God: command deliver-
> ances for Jacob. Through thee will we push down our
> enemies: through thy name will we tread them under that
> rise up against us.

It is through Christ that we are strong. It is He who delivers us, who fights for us, who rescues and redeems us, who shelters and protects us, who provides for our needs, who guides our feet.

May we always remember what God has done for us, that we do not lose sight of those things when going through fiery trials. May we allow ourselves to be humbled by the trials God allows in our lives, and turn to Him as the only source, the only way out.

To view lyrics for songs referenced in this chapter,
please visit http://songdove.fa-ct.com/
There you will find interactive Scripture references, videos containing lyrics to
most of the songs listed here, topics mentioned in this chapter, and more.

Scriptures used, referred to or that relate to thoughts in this session:

Psalm 44   Job 13:14   Micah 7:7-10

Songs shared, referenced, or that relate to thoughts in this session:

Trading My Sorrows   Cry Out to Jesus

Topics discussed, referred to, or that relate to thoughts in this session:

Failure   Chastisement
Shame   Trust
Surrender   Finances
Forgiveness   Fear of man
Humility

Questions for Discussion:

What situations have caused shame in your own life?

_____

_____

When you look back over those situations, were/are there opportunities for
growth, lessons, or humbling before God or others? Brainstorm a little. . .

_____

_____

When does shame lead us to God? _____

_____

Is there such a thing as healthy versus unhealthy shame? Explain:

_____

_____

Trading My Sorrows
CCLI Song No. 2574653
© 1998 Integrity's Hosanna! Music
Darrell Evans

Cry Out To Jesus
CCLI Song No. 4586106
© 2005 Consuming Fire Music (Admin. by EMI Christian Music Publishing)
Brad Avery | David Carr | Mac Powell | Mark Lee | Tai Anderson

A Desire of Every Woman

> **Psalm 3:3** But thou, O LORD, *art* a shield for me; my glory, and the lifter up of mine head.

This echoes my thoughts of God being the lifter of my head, of lifting my eyes to see His, of the song we sing pleading to see His face as we desire His power and love to fall on us. . .

What every woman wants in a man is what God offers Himself. . . power under control displayed through intimate gentle love made evident through His eyes and His touch. . . The image of the strong male figure who fights for his lady and after the battle takes her into his arms in a display of intimacy that makes her all but faint in his embrace. . . Christ did this, taking on the forces of Satan through His death and resurrection, and turning around to embrace a lover who many times doesn't think He's capable of such intimate behaviour. . .

That He took our place on the cross and that He now seeks, desires, and longs for intimacy with His hard-won Bride reminds me of a movie I saw a long time ago. It was called "A Town Called Alice" and took place during World War II and the years following. In this movie, a lady and her friends got rounded up for what would later be called the million man (or was it mile) march. . . also called death marches. Mostly women and children made up the crew of prisoners in this march, and a few men. An Australian man saw the woman who we'd learn was the main character in this story, and took it upon himself to make sure her needs were met throughout the march, stealing from the soldiers' tents to feed her and her friends, bringing them water when the guards weren't looking, etc. He was caught a few times, and after one particularly daring attempt to meet her need for food, he was whipped badly on his back, causing huge welts to rise up. This woman made it to the march's destination and a few years later, moved to Australia as part of her job. The man recognized her but she did not recognize him. They fell in love and went to a beach side cabin for the summer. The movie ends as he is sitting on the cabin steps looking out at the water, and she comes out of the cabin as he removes his shirt. At that moment she sees the scars, still very large on his back. The movie faded out as she sat down beside him with a new-found love and amazement for the man who had risked so much for her safety back when she hardly knew who he was.

> **Romans 5:8** But God commendeth his love toward us, in that, while we were yet sinners, Christ died for us.

Christ did this for me. . . on the death march of sin. . . He took it upon Himself to see to it that my needs were met and took my punishment upon Himself, defeating the chains of death, setting me free. . . but while I accepted this gift of salvation and forgiveness of sin years ago, it wasn't till the spring of '07 that I was ready to respond to Him desperately, longingly, intimately, desiring the passion He'd introduce me to in such an unforgettable manner. . .

> **John 20:27** Then saith he to Thomas, Reach hither thy finger, and behold my hands; and reach hither thy hand, and thrust it into my side: and be not faithless, but believing.

He still bears the scars of payment for my freedom. . . He asked Thomas to touch them. . . bearing them in his glorified form!!!

How much more romantic can you get than choosing to bear the scars that freed your lover from her imminent eternal death? He could have wiped them out at the moment of His resurrection. There was no need to maintain in glorified form what He'd suffered for our sakes. . . But He chose to bear such a reminder. . . surely not for His own sake, as being God there is no such thing as memory loss. He knows all things past present and future. . . but that we'd see His scars and fall in love with Him all over again with hearts so heavy with gratitude that only His intimate touch would satisfy the longing, the desperation, the need to be surrounded in His loving arms. . .

> **John 15:13** Greater love hath no man than this, that a man lay down his life for his friends.

How can we not fall in love with One who paid such a high price for our rescue? The Bride of Christ, God's most prize creation, was the famed damsel in distress. . . only issue is. . . many members of humanity don't see themselves as being in any sort of distress. Christ saw she who would become His Bride, in desperate need of salvation from sin's slippery slope to hell, and willingly came to her rescue. . . paying the death penalty in her place.

The Singing Saviour

> **Zephaniah 3:17** The LORD thy God in the midst of thee is mighty; he will save, he will rejoice over thee with joy; he will rest in his love, he will joy over thee with singing.

> **Psalm 32:7** Thou *art* my hiding place; thou shalt preserve me from trouble; thou shalt compass me about with songs of deliverance. Selah.

I need look no further for One who will fight for me than Jesus Christ Himself. . . He loves me enough to fight for me, and not only does He fight for me, but He rejoices over me with songs of deliverance!!!

My unseen Husband sings over me. . . He fights for me, He took my punishment, He gave me new clothes of His own righteousness, He washed away my sin, He lifts my head, and He gazes into the eyes of my heart with such soft, intense, deep, intimate, passionate, caring love. . . such a thought makes my heart ask if it's OK to pass out now. . . That He chose to come alongside as my unseen Husband in addition to all this, meeting me so intimately. . . I can't help but long for Him, to long for His touch, to sense His passionate love for me. . . to see His face, to see His eyes. . .

To view lyrics for songs referenced in this chapter,
please visit http://songdove.fa-ct.com/
There you will find interactive Scripture references, videos containing lyrics to most of the songs listed here, topics mentioned in this chapter, and more.

Scriptures used, referred to or that relate to thoughts in this session:

Psalm 3:3	John 20:27	Zephaniah 3:17
Romans 5:8	John 15:13	Psalm 32:7

Songs shared, referenced, or that relate to thoughts in this session:

Hallelujah (Your Love Makes Me Sing)

Topics discussed, referred to, or that relate to thoughts in this session:

God's Love	Bride of Christ
Our Response	Rescue from Sin

Questions for Discussion:

Does God love you? Yes_____ No _____ How do you know?

_____

_____

What did Christ say to Thomas?

_____

_____

Why do you think Christ maintained the scars of His ordeal?

_____

_____

Finish the verse: "Greater love hath no man than this, _____

_____

Write out Zephaniah 3:17 below:

_____

_____

_____

_____

Hallelujah

CCLI Song No. 3091812
© 2000 Vineyard Songs (UK/Eire) (Admin. by Vineyard Music UK)
Brenton Brown | Brian Doerksen

Eyes

> **Proverbs 4:20-21** My son, attend to my words; incline thine
> ear unto my sayings. ²¹Let them not depart from thine eyes;
> keep them in the midst of thine heart.

Eyes are how I see the soul of a person, eyes are how I can almost see a person's thoughts. Sunglasses sometimes frustrate me because I am prevented from seeing deep into who I am speaking with. . . Indeed I firmly believe that the eyes are the window to the soul. . . and perhaps God does too. How often do we see references to the eyes of our heart, or to God's eyes? We sing of opening the eyes of our heart that we might see God. . . and what part of God have I said I personally see? Almost as if I can see His eyes, such tender, deep, intense, intimate eyes. . .

If this is what it's like now when I can't literally see Him in front of me and can't physically feel His arms around me. . . what will it be like in Heaven? To finally see my Saviour, finally see the Lover of my soul, to finally meet my Creator and King face to face. . . The Prince of Peace came for me. . . such a story of royal hard-fought love. . . Sometimes I think the greater battle isn't defeating Satan and his minions through His death and resurrection, but winning over the love of the very princess He fought for. . . Again I wonder what it must be like to have fought for a bride who doesn't think her groom can love her intimately or passionately but who merely loves her by way of service and provision.

A Prayer
Oh my God, may I never see You that way ever again. . . May I never be drawn away from this place of intimate contact. . . Oh God. . .
***

"How can I keep from Singing", by Chris Tomlin, began playing the night I first wrote these words.

I guess it's just the fact that in spite of my humanity and all its frailties, mistakes, regrets, etc, that God's love continues toward me unabated. . . It continues to hit me with fresh gratitude, fresh amazement, and fresh thankfulness. I don't deserve what God has extended to me. . . God met me with another hug and while the physical touch wasn't there, as in knocking up against another skin or muscle, there was a sense on my arms like a muted contact with static electricity that lifts your arm hairs. . . So close to being tangible! I feel something similar as I type these words. One of the ladies in my prayer group says God meets her like this when she's driving occasionally. God is so amazing. . .

> **Ephesians 2:8-9** For by grace are ye saved through faith; and that not of yourselves: it is the gift of God: [9]Not of works, lest any man should boast.

But an underlying yet emphatic theme through all of this has been that my own efforts and my own mistakes don't affect this love Christ has for me. With all the feelings of failure and the various times I've felt like crawling in a hole, God still extends His love to me so unconditionally, so non-judgmentally, so accepting. . . Once again it's not because of anything I've done, not done, could or couldn't do, it was entirely because of how He sees me through His own righteousness given on the Cross of Calvary. This repeated realization is going to stay with me for awhile as I realize afresh, over and over again, that while no one is harder on me than I am, that no one is as loving and as accepting of me as Christ is. I continue to be amazed at how Christ has had others model this to me. I've given them various opportunities to drop me and walk away, but instead they've built me up in the eyes of others and encouraged my participation in ministry, even standing by in prayer and moral support when needed. I can't thank them enough for that! Nor am I able to adequately express my thanks and amazement to God for birthing that level of acceptance in them.

To view lyrics for songs referenced in this chapter,
please visit http://songdove.fa-ct.com/
There you will find interactive Scripture references, videos containing lyrics to
most of the songs listed here, topics mentioned in this chapter, and more.

Scriptures used, referred to or that relate to thoughts in this session:

Ephesians 2:8-9   Proverbs 4:20-21   Proverbs 23:26

2 Chronicles 16:9   Proverbs 15:30

Songs shared, referenced, or that relate to thoughts in this session:

How Can I Keep From Singing   Open the Eyes of My Heart Lord

Topics discussed, referred to, or that relate to thoughts in this session:

Eyes of the heart   Efforts

Seeing God   Relationship with God not physical

Acceptance   Unconditional Love

Questions for Discussion:

"Eyes are the _____ to the _____"

What verses seem to back up that saying above? Why or how?

_____

God's love is conditional. True _____ False _____ How do you know?

_____

What is meant by "Eyes of the heart?" Use the Scriptures for help with this
answer.

_____

_____

How Can I Keep From Singing

CCLI Song No. 4822372

© 2006 worshiptogether.com songs | sixsteps Music | Alletrop Music | Thankyou Music | Vamos Publishing (Admin. by EMI Christian Music Publishing) | (Admin. by EMI Christian Music Publishing) | (Admin. by Music Services, Inc.) | (Admin. by EMI Christian Music Publishing) | (Admin. by EMI Christian Music Publishing)

Chris Tomlin | Ed Cash | Matt Redman

Open The Eyes Of My Heart

CCLI Song No. 2298355

© 1997 Integrity's Hosanna! Music (Admin. by EMI Christian Music Publishing)

Paul Baloche

This author struggles with self-acceptance.

> **Romans 5:8** But God commendeth his love toward us, in that, while we were yet sinners, Christ died for us.

Thank goodness God isn't rushing the self-acceptance thing! Others have had encouraging things to say and admonishments as I travel down a road I should have travelled long ago. It's hard not to feel a certain level of self-condemnation and regret even as my daughter begins to talk about how she sees other girls dressing, accessorizing or doing hair and makeup. She currently has a healthy attitude about herself, to accept herself as God made her and that how He made her is perfectly okay with her. I'd tried to foster this early in her life, totally unaware that I'd lost sight of this for myself.

The picture of Christ's acceptance for me as portrayed in the book , "Song of Songs: Journey of the Bride" (see website for this resource in chapter 1), is something I am discovering I have been longing for. Not just His acceptance, but His incredibly unconditional love!!! So many times I fail, fail my children, fail my clients, fail my boss, fail my own expectations of myself. Sometimes I even feel like I'm failing God as I struggle with various issues involved in being a single parent trying to live as God's asked of me when so many around me ignore what God's said in Scripture and come up with justifications to appease these desires in their own lives. I have feelings. I have dreams. I have desires. I have longings, and as much as I try to transport them over to Christ, there is still something. . . I hate to put it like this, as if God can't meet all desires. . . but something. . . missing!

There is the human interaction element God built into mankind, forms of interaction that so far I am not experiencing in this new place in His love for me. There are certain things that I guess just can't be attributed to God in any way shape or form. That doesn't explain how some people say they are so full of God that they honestly don't desire anyone of the opposite gender. So I find myself asking if I should seek out that level of intimacy and interaction with my God, or if I should be asking that my children and I be freed so I can find them a new dad. These thoughts at times make me feel as if I'm failing God by not finding 100% fulfilment in His embrace. Yet for all these perceived failures, Christ still looks at me with deep, caring, loving eyes, and when I'm allowed to see those eyes, I see a depth of sincerity, of a deep-seated love that makes me wish I could disappear into them. How could anyone accept me so unconditionally?

1 John 4:19 We love him, because he first loved us.

We have an amazing God! The way Simmons keeps describing Christ's love in relation to the **Song of Solomon**, would seem to say that it doesn't matter if we love Him of our own choosing, but that we simply respond to His continual wooing, of His repeated request to be allowed to love the rough spots out of our lives, that He sees us for who we are capable of being, not for what sin has done to mar us. Now this does confirm Scriptures in the New Testament regarding how He loved us first, that our love is born out of response to His love toward us.

Part of the perception of failure, is the expectation of others.

Expectations

I know I mess up as much as I try to move forward, but that's just part of the maturing process. I must ask my reader to forgive me for any time I come across wrong as I share this journey. I'm trying. . . Part of me wants to be told whenever I could improve on things interpersonally, but part of me is scared if too many people give me such feedback that I'll destroy myself again as I try to meet expectations from too many sources. I got myself fired from a job because I got stressed out over trying to be what others expected of me and "lost it" with a fellow employee in front of customers one night. I knew my job was gone before the boss told me it was gone. Ever since then I've tried to avoid asking people for feedback on how I should or shouldn't live inter-personally. But at the same time, if there's something glaring, and if someone not only tells me what's wrong but gives practical ways of going about improving the situation, I value the input. What drives me around the bend is someone pointing out that something could change, but doesn't offer practical ways to bring about the change.

What about Me?

At the same time I hear Christ saying in that quiet way "what about Me?" If I don't think too much about His status in Heaven, if I just focus on who He is intimately and personally, I have no problem with asking Him for hugs, with desiring His intimate presence. But if I start contrasting that to His greatness, to His powerfulness, to His position of Creator and King of Kings, it just blows me away all over again that He'd want to embrace me, would choose to die for me, would want me as His Bride. Indeed, "what about Him?" His opinion of me matters more than anyone else in the whole wide world, His view of what I am and how I can improve. The best part being that to effect the changes God asks for, the biggest effort is in the surrendering and submitting to His efforts in my life. It isn't me striving to make changes on my own, but God effecting those changes in me as I surrender to His control in my life.

Indeed His love is amazing! That I could never earn this love, never impact it, that Christ offers it to me freely, not just once, but repeatedly to gently drive home the message that it doesn't matter how many times I fail, He loves me anyway!!! Doesn't that make you want to embrace Him for yourself??? How can we not respond to such love? How can we remain cold to this unconditional, all-encompassing, forgiving, patient, deeply caring love?

"Your love makes me sing" by Brenton Brown played again as I wrote this!

The love I have for my King didn't start with me, a thought that still slams my inclination for independent feeling toward others. Those lyrics came so timely! Truly music is the love language where I exchange communication with my God!

To view lyrics for songs referenced in this chapter,
please visit http://songdove.fa-ct.com/
There you will find interactive Scripture references, videos containing lyrics to
most of the songs listed here, topics mentioned in this chapter, and more.

Scriptures used, referred to or that relate to thoughts in this session:

1 John 4:9-19   Romans 5:8

Songs shared, referenced, or that relate to thoughts in this session:

Hallelujah(Your Love Makes Me Sing)

Topics discussed, referred to, or that relate to thoughts in this session:

Seeing God   Relationship with God not physical
Acceptance   Unconditional Love
Failure

Questions for Discussion:

Whose opinion matters most to you? Be honest here. Why?

_____

_____

Using the topical search in chapter 3 on the website or the nearest Strong's
Concordance, what other Scriptures can you find about God's unconditional
love?

_____

_____

Who loved who first? Us or God? _____

How does God see us? How does that make you feel?

_____

_____

Have you ever struggled with self-acceptance? How has God helped you through?

_____

_____

_____

_____

Hallelujah

CCLI Song No. 3091812
© 2000 Vineyard Songs (UK/Eire) (Admin. by Vineyard Music UK)
Brenton Brown | Brian Doerksen

Restoration and Old/New Beginnings

> **2 Corinthians 5:17** Therefore if any man be in Christ, he is a new creature: old things are passed away; behold, all things are become new.

> **John 15:1-5** I am the true vine, and my Father is the husbandman. ²Every branch in me that beareth not fruit he taketh away: and every branch that beareth fruit, he purgeth it, that it may bring forth more fruit. ³Now ye are clean through the word which I have spoken unto you. ⁴Abide in me, and I in you. As the branch cannot bear fruit of itself, except it abide in the vine; no more can ye, except ye abide in me. ⁵I am the vine, ye are the branches: He that abideth in me, and I in him, the same bringeth forth much fruit: for without me ye can do nothing.

I look at life before the Fall of 2006, then look at life since March of 2007, and the way God's doing things seems so new. It's as if I had to go through a pruning where it seemed everything I was ever used to doing was all but stripped from me minus my ability to sing before the Lord. Along with the stripping came new ways of ministering to the local Body, taking over the music ministry website for the benefit of my worship pastor (at the time) and team members, discovering myself actually conducting a choir (!).

Since that storm broke, it seems that God is reviving, refreshing, and rebuilding giftings, talents and abilities that I could have sworn I used to move in before, but in ways I don't remember in times past. As if He had to take these things, and like a doctor re-breaks a bone that healed wrong to reset its position to heal properly, God had to break off what He'd given me and give it back how it was supposed to be positioned in my life. Everything in this area of life seems so new as result. Old but new, in a way that feels like rediscovery.

Life before the storm seems so far away now. The storm looks like an impenetrable dark cloud in some ways, making it hard to see some of the things I used to remember being part of. Talking about how I used to be in these areas now seems so selfish. I don't remember being active in God's House for selfish reasons before, although during my marriage it did become an escape from my home life. But. . . it's a new day, a new chapter, it feels like God is redesigning, repositioning, rebuilding and reteaching me both in and for this new chapter in my life.

From Goat-Keeper to Queen, Rags to Riches

Going through Song of Solomon as I read "Song of Songs: Journey of the Bride", I discovered it is indeed the journey of the Shulamite from goat-keeper to queen that I identify with, not so much the wording of the book itself after all. It's her attitudes, her feelings, her desires and how they change as the King continually calls and woos her.

Then there is the Moabitess in the book of Ruth, and how her commitment and dedication lead her into a path of humbling herself to glean and how she goes from a gleaner to the mother that began the lineage that would bring us Jesus' earthly parents! Now that's a rags to riches story if there ever was one!!!

From goats to queen, from gleaning to great-great grandmother of King David, upon whose throne God promised a King forever! Rahab has this story too, in the book of Joshua, from prostitute to acceptance in Israel (**Joshua 6:25**).

All three of these women come from outside the Kingdom, from outside the Chosen people. Through their obedience, their submission, their humbleness and their surrender, they become grafted into the tree that would one day bring me my personal loving Saviour! I would encourage the reader to read the stories of these three women.

It isn't so much that they are female so much, as their paths from rags to riches, from lowliness to positions of respect, why they were where they started, and how they got to where they ended up.

Carried to the Table

The story of Mephibosheth too, in 2 Samuel 9, is a story of a young man, lame in both feet, who through no ability of his own, earns the favour of King David simply by his association as grandson to King Saul, being of the family of Jonathan. In many ways this is yet another example of this path I speak of. That through nothing we could do on our own, but through association with Jesus Christ, we are brought into the Throne Room of Almighty God, embraced as sons, and called the Bride of Christ! A song that illustrates this concept so beautifully is by Leeland. "Carried to the Table".

To view lyrics for songs referenced in this chapter,
please visit http://songdove.fa-ct.com/
There you will find interactive Scripture references, videos containing lyrics to most of the songs listed here, topics mentioned in this chapter, and more.

Scriptures used, referred to or that relate to thoughts in this session:

Song of Solomon	Genesis 37-45	John 15:1-5
Joshua 6:25	2 Samuel 9	
Ruth	2 Corinthians 5:17	

Songs shared, referenced, or that relate to thoughts in this session:

Carried to the Table

Topics discussed, referred to, or that relate to thoughts in this session:

Seeing God	Storms of Life
Acceptance	Being Broken
Failure	Response
Relationship with God not physical	Humility
Unconditional Love	

Questions for Discussion:

What Rags to Riches stories can you recount from Scripture?

_____

_____

There's one story that begins in Genesis 37. Who is it and what did they have to endure on their way to where God wanted them?

_____

_____

Where are you on your Rags to Riches story?

_____

_____

The Shulamite, Ruth, Mephibosheth, Rahab, and Joseph all had one thing in common. I'll give you a big hint. . . Something to do with effort.

_____

_____

Who loved who first? Us or God? _____

How does God see us? How does that make you feel?

_____

_____

Using the topical search in chapter 3 on the website or the nearest Strong's Concordance,, what other Scriptures can you find about God's unconditional love?

_____

_____

Have you ever struggled with self-acceptance? How has God helped you through?

_____

_____

_____

_____

What does God's pruning/purging look like in the life of the Christian?

_____

_____

Carried to the Table

CCLI Song No. 4681678
© Meaux Mercy | Meaux Hits | Colorwheel Songs | Blue Raft Music (Admin. by EMI Christian Music Publishing)
Leeland Mooring | Marc Byrd | Steve Hindalong

Loneliness, Rejection and God

> **Psalm 46:10** Be still, and know that I am God: I will be exalted among the heathen, I will be exalted in the earth.

"Be Still", by Storyside B, talks about loneliness and how God is there in our loneliness.

The kaleidoscope that is this journey continues to intensify. I very quickly discovered early on, that some concepts can't be talked about or understood without other concepts being solidly woven in such an intricate mix that it was difficult sorting them out for the purposes of putting this on paper!

Vulnerability Alert:

It's when I slow down that I find myself longing for friends. As long as there's no one out there who wants to spend time with me, I don't know that I'll want to be slowing down. With no one to share with, slow times are times of introspection and musings, and while some of it is healthy, I can't claim it all is, and some of it is downright self-destructive in an emotional sense. But just the same, it's in those slow times that I sense God's intimate presence too. He's always got time for me. I actually crawl into bed these days, lay my head on the pillow and tell God, "OK, God, I'm here now", and so often it's as if He responds with one of those intangible hugs, a sense of loving comfort comes over me as if I'm literally in His embrace, resting my head on His chest. That's been soooo needed at the end of some days.

The subject one night at Beth Moore's "Living Beyond Yourself" Bible Study, turned out to be on rejection, and how if we do not let God heal its wounds in our lives, we can end up doing things to assuage it that we never thought we'd ever do, such as taking revenge or allowing relationships into our lives that aren't healthy. The examples Beth Moore used to illustrate various types of rejection didn't ring any bells for me initially. But just the same I felt something that she didn't talk about. . . feelings of rejection borne out of loneliness.

I found myself subduing tears as I realized that one of the reasons I fear rejection is because of fearing a deeper loneliness. The loner in me now finds being alone a threat, a spectre, and things I do and say are sometimes gauged now by whether I will gain or lose relationships that matter very deeply to me.

It's as if. . . I rejected myself! Is that possible??? If I have never experienced the pain of a parent kicking me out of the family, if I have never had a spouse walk out on me, why else would I fear this? My first boyfriend left me, yes, that was rejection, but we were friends for a few years after that. Dad never outright rejected me, it was his treatment of me and my efforts in various areas of life that caused me to feel that way. But I know that after I left my ex, I personally got scared. . . scared I wouldn't be accepted in ministry again. . . This fear was founded in old Pentecostal behaviour toward divorcees that no longer takes place. But because I had this fear, I felt others would look at me the same way, and if they did, that would mean rejection in the very areas of life that matter most to me.

Phantoms in the Mind

My experience of rejection then isn't real, it's a phantom, it's a "what if" fear, not a "this really happened" memory with a resulting wound. The other phantom in my life is the logical sister to loneliness, schedules. Loneliness suggests people don't want to be around me. Schedules dictate time availability, so the hint that I'm alone because people don't want to be around me is false.

The Beth Moore study's daily portions between video segments were focusing on God's agape love. How it's only through the Holy Spirit that we can show this kind of love toward people. . . Clearly, being able to love others in a way that won't destroy them is something I seem incapable of on my own, that even there, whether its friendship love, brotherly love, agape love, or intimate love, I need God doing it through me.

This line of thought one night was an unwelcome surprise. . . wanting to learn how to let God's love flow through me toward others was not some-

thing I anticipated having to cross the hurdle of rejection over. But Beth's right, I have to overcome this if I am to become the conduit I desire to be, even if the fear of rejection is a phantom in my mind and not real, created by my own failed expectations of myself rather than having failed anyone else's. .
.

To view lyrics for songs referenced in this chapter,
please visit http://songdove.fa-ct.com/
There you will find interactive Scripture references, videos containing lyrics to most of the songs listed here, topics mentioned in this chapter, and more.

Scriptures used, referred to or that relate to thoughts in this session:

Psalm 46:10   See Chapter 8 online for verses on God's Strength in our weakness

Songs shared, referenced, or that relate to thoughts in this session:

Be Still

Topics discussed, referred to, or that relate to thoughts in this session:

Rejection   God's Agape Love
Relationship with God and mankind Holy Spirit displaying love through us
(No physical contact)
"What If" Fears

Questions for Discussion:

What fears has the enemy plagued you with?

_____

_____

Are these fears real or phantom?

_____

Be Still
Storyside "B"

Lyrical Lessons

I would direct my reader to the companion website, to chapter 3's page and find the song "Through the Fire". Listen to the lyrics as you consider what I've just written to this point. I chuckle over how true to my story this song's lyrics are! I couldn't help shaking my head at times when our choir was learning it, and going "ooooh man. . .". Indeed that is one song I can sing from the heart. How hard is it for me to act without answers??? And yet He has always gone through everything with me if all I'll do is submit, surrender, obey, and step forward. *sigh*. . . Those I trust have seen me through so much of this. . . It was powerful when we finally presented this song!

Dealing with Failure in Loneliness as Lyrical Lessons Continue

"My Saviour's Love (I Stand Amazed)" was in the song set picked for one particular Sunday morning. . . What were the chances I got through that service without tears, a raining heart at the very least? Tears of gratitude, amazement, and the threat of pouring out a heart that continues to break so easily. I continue to be shown that God is the One I need to be turning to for so many things that I used to think He gave us other humans for. I laid my head on my pillow one night, closed my eyes, and asked God if it was OK to get a hug. I could almost imagine the touch of a hand cupping my face and leaning it toward an unseen chest. Sometimes His presence can seem so close to being tangible, as if He allows Himself to be felt. . . in that manner where I'm tempted to reach out and touch what ends up being thin air. But if I don't try to reach out, if I just accept the input to my senses He seems to allow occasionally, He seems so close, so intimately close.

I know my past has played a big part in why I fall into moments of abandoned worship so easily. How can I not long to be close to the heart of One who has loved me so unconditionally, who has seen fit to restore me in ways I never dreamed of in years past, who not only saved my soul, but comes close to me?

> **Micah 7:8-10** Rejoice not against me, O mine enemy: when I fall, I shall arise; when I sit in darkness, the LORD *shall be* a light unto me. [9]I will bear the indignation of the LORD, because I have sinned against him, until he plead my cause, and execute judgment for me: he will bring me forth to the light, *and* I shall behold his righteousness. [10]Then *she that is* mine enemy shall see *it,* and shame shall cover her which said unto me, Where is the LORD thy God? mine eyes shall behold her: now shall she be trodden down as the mire of the streets.

Pastor once shared in a sermon to appropriate the sufficiency of Christ, and declare to the enemy the above verses, then share with a friend. . . As if to illustrate this, "Only Grace" comes on Praise106.5 as I type, as if God Himself is wishing for me to recognize and indeed appropriate His sufficiency through Christ. I don't take it lightly that these songs come on just when such thoughts are afflicting me. This song in particular seems to come on almost every single time I fight with thoughts of shame and condemnation.

sigh I probably should have responded to that sermon that Sunday. "Arms of Love", "Your Beloved", "I Believe", "Great God", "All Things Are Possible". . . Our worship pastor was preaching a sermon of his own that morning!!! Completely and totally complimenting Pastor's, and confirmed by Word of Knowledge that same morning!

My heart gets to longing as I consider the two messages. . . I know it was wrong to run from my feelings that morning, my justification in some ways was pretty shallow. I just didn't want to ruin my daughter's birthday party that afternoon so I hid and didn't go forward. (Emotions can take a bit to calm down)

But just as "Only Grace" sings, "if you should fall, get up again", Pastor showing in Micah where the prophet declares that though he falls, he will rise again. . . I feel in my spirit that this means not to wallow in how I'm feeling, but to indeed get up again. However I am getting the distinct impression that getting up again is not to be done on my own strength, but to allow God to raise me up, to pick me up, apply His healing balm and set me on my feet again.

These bouts of shame, fear of rejection, isolation, fear of hurting others, can go for months without plaguing me. But it seems they come flooding back whenever loneliness hits, as if they are being used by the enemy as "reasons" for my loneliness, flogging me with them. It's hard not to believe them.

To view lyrics for songs referenced in this chapter,
please visit http://songdove.fa-ct.com/
There you will find interactive Scripture references, videos containing lyrics to most of the songs listed here, topics mentioned in this chapter, and more.

Scriptures used, referred to or that relate to thoughts in this session:

Micah 7:8-10	See Chapter 8 online for verses on God's
Romans 5:8	Strength in our weakness

Songs shared, referenced, or that relate to thoughts in this session:

Through the Fire	Your Beloved
My Saviour's Love	I Believe
Only Grace	Great God
Arms of Love	All Things Are Possible

Topics discussed, referred to, or that relate to thoughts in this session:

Loneliness	God's Agape Love
Relationship with God and mankind	God's Strength
(No physical contact)	

Questions for Discussion:

How can Micah 7:8-10 be applied when your fears knock you down?

_____

_____

Where do you long for God's Strength to help you get back up on your feet?

_____

_____

Arms Of Love
CCLI Song No. 824481© 1991 Mercy / Vineyard Publishing | Vineyard Songs Canada | ION Publishing (Admin. by Music Services, Inc.) | (Admin. by Music Services, Inc.) | (Admin. by Music Services, Inc.)
Craig Musseau

Through the Fire
Gerald Crabb. © 1999 Lehsem Songs

I Stand Amazed
CCLI Song No. 25297
© Public Domain
Charles Hutchison Gabriel

Only Grace
CCLI Song No. 4256144
© 2005 Word Music, LLC | Westies, Inc. Music Publishing | Greenberg Music (a div. of Word Music Group, Inc.) | (Admin. by Word Music Group, Inc.) | (Admin. by Bug Music, Inc.)
Kenny Greenberg | Matthew West

Your Beloved
CCLI Song No. 1963849
© 1996 Mercy / Vineyard Publishing (Admin. by Music Services, Inc.)
Brent Helming

You Are My King (Amazing Love)

CCLI Song No. 2456623
© 1996 worshiptogether.com songs (Admin. by EMI Christian Music Publishing)
Billy Foote

I Believe

CCLI Song No. 2808824
© 1998, 2000 Vineyard Songs Canada | ION Publishing (Admin. by Music Services, Inc.) |
(Admin. by Music Services, Inc.)
Graham Ord

Great God

CCLI Song No. 1858786
© 1996 Vineyard Songs Canada | ION Publishing (Admin. by Music Services) | (Admin. by
Vineyard Music USA)
David Wilding

All Things Are Possible

CCLI Song No. 2245140
© 1997 Hillsong Publishing (Admin. by EMI Christian Music Publishing)
Darlene Zschech

Forgiveness

Progression along this journey has brought me face to face with the fact that one issue is the matter of forgiving myself, even more than being assured of God's forgiveness. I invite my reader into my head as God presented me with a lesson as I wrote out my struggle in this area. By now you will be aware that at times, what you are reading sounds more like that of a journal or letter than the traditional prose of a book or devotional. What follows continues in that style.

The shame and condemnation that attacks me at times wouldn't be there if I could somehow find it within myself to actually forgive me, myself. I am so full of thankfulness and gratitude for all that Christ has done for me. I over-flow with gratitude for all He's done through others to me too.

One lady echoed my own comments about needing to forgive myself. She was talking to a mutual friend who had told her that to not forgive ourselves is to spite God's forgiveness, to somehow claim that God's gift of salvation and atoning work on the Cross was insufficient! I looked at her and internally said "ouch"!!!

I continually find it so amazing how quickly God speaks to my thoughts and realizations at times! This time just hours after I commented how I think the weekend's torture could have been alleviated if I'd just reach a point of self-forgiveness. . . Then the self-forgiveness issue gets confirmed and isn't even part of the study, it's just a pre-study comment by one of the ladies at my table!!!

These thoughts on forgiveness came during a very difficult time when shame for wrong decisions weighed heavily upon me! I share this struggle here, not because I've arrived and have reached complete and full self-forgiveness in all areas of my life, but to show that God was there even in my wonderings and struggles over the issue.

Sometimes that's all God wants, for us to give voice to honest questions, to ponder the things He speaks to us about, and to have open hearts to what He desires to do.

I reached a point in the first 6 months of my journey, when how God was moving in my life blew me out of the water! God had swooped in so decidedly, that I couldn't help the following outburst!

I feel like asking a really dumb question! They say there are no dumb questions, but this one is. . . What did I do, how did I ever earn this kind of treatment??? That God would show up so instantly these days??? Answering my questions before anyone even sees them??? Confirming thoughts going around my head so quickly. . . Is it just that I'm finally listening, finally responding, finally desiring the things He desires for me??? Is it possible my ears have finally opened. . . That it took that awful storm to open them??? Or is it simply Him very much enacting the role of unseen Husband by noticeably showing up everywhere I go now, bringing out questions, comments, songs, Scripture, confirmations of various sorts to assure me that I'm not out in left field, that I'm hearing and asking correctly???

The answer is to somehow bring myself to the same state of forgiving myself that Christ was at on the Cross. . . If God thought He could forgive me, who am I to do otherwise??? Talk about a twist on the ungrateful servant story in **Matthew 18:21-34**, eh? In this case it isn't me going to someone else and demanding they pay all, being unforgiving, it's me going to myself and doing that! So. . . is this simply a matter of accepting all over again what Christ did on the Cross and applying it to the choices that were responsible for my black blot? Is this a matter of. . . this sounds really bad. . . but a matter of "lowering" my bar, my level of expectation of how things should have been, to the level God's is on??? Is it possible to have higher standards for myself than God does??? In some ways I'm glad God's expectations when seen through the lens of Christ's righteousness, do seem lower than my own. God is far more forgiving of me than I am, quite clearly.

Job 11:6 That He would show you the secrets of wisdom! For they would double your prudence. Know therefore that God exacts from you less than your iniquity deserves.

Romans 5:8 But God commendeth his love toward us, in that, while we were yet sinners, Christ died for us.

I see what I deserve, the choices I made. . .Scripture says that while I was still in sin, God loved me. . . I could have been damned to hell, but God chose to offer me Salvation. . . chose to show mercy and grace. . .Each time I sin, He is so quick to offer forgiveness when I come in repentance and sorrow. . . But how many times have I refused to offer this to myself?

I am guilty of holding over my head a judgement God has removed from me, as if what He lovingly did was wrong, a mistake, ill-thought out. . . Truly there is a danger of thinking that we are beyond forgiveness! If that were the case, then Christ's death on the Cross was in vain and God's omniscience and omnipotence are nothing more than facades and charades! This is of course, a lie, as far from the truth as my sin is from my Father's mind.

The verse in Job above was like a finger in my face when I first came across it. God exacts from me far less than what my iniquity deserves. . . so far less that He sees me standing in the robes of righteousness given me by Jesus Christ. . . who am I to say that my wrongs can't be forgiven???

Allow me, dear reader, another moment of vulnerability before you and God. I, as much as anyone who has ever faced circumstances requiring their self-forgiveness, need to work through this. . . I've suffered bouts of shame ever since I fled my ex. I've suffered bouts of condemnation ever since I left him. Reaching that place of forgiving myself as Christ forgave me is getting easier and I know that once I do that, Satan doesn't have that tool anymore and can't flog me like he has.

This has been confirmed to me by several people since. God still wants to touch me there. I can feel it. I am so not used to the gentle way He addresses things in my life. He'd begun the gentle treatment through my mentor a year before my new chapter began, and continued it, not only through my mentor, but directly from Himself as well. We have such an awesome God!

A Prayer

Oh my Lord. . . oh my God. . . my Redeemer, Saviour. . . forgive me for refusing to forgive myself. . . I've let it go for so long thinking that I can't forgive myself, that it's so hard to do. Oh God, I've let my choices torture me for too long. . . oh my Jesus. . . I ask for the ability to forgive myself, to release myself from my past. . . oh Lord, forgive me for this sin of unforgiveness. . . Help me to see myself as You see me, to see my failures as You see them, through Your eyes of mercy, through Your eyes of grace. . . oh God, I don't want to lose the awe, the wonder, the amazement, the gratitude toward all that You've done and continue to do in my life since I made the choices that weigh me down so heavily at times. I just want to be free of the guilt and shame that has hung on for so long. Free me Father, show me how to free myself, and I ask for the means beyond myself to do this. . .Oh Lord. . . in Jesus' name. . .
***

To read Scriptures referenced in this chapter,
please visit http://songdove.fa-ct.com/
There you will find interactive Scripture references, videos containing lyrics to most of the songs in these chapters, topics mentioned in this chapter, and more.

Scriptures used, referred to or that relate to thoughts in this session:

Matthew 18:21-34	Romans 5:8
Job 11:6	

Topics discussed, referred to, or that relate to thoughts in this session:

Forgiveness	God's Strength
Self-Forgiveness	Disarming the Enemy
God's Agape Love	

Questions for Discussion:

Do you struggle with self-forgiveness? Yes_____ No_____ If yes, care to share?

_____

_____

How does Job 11:6 come across to you?

_____

_____

Who knows better, us or God? Explain.

_____

_____

How does God see us?

_____

_____

Noticing Changes

I don't know about you dear reader, but as I progress along this journey, the feeling of a kid in a candy store has given way to that of feeling like I'm in an adventure park instead. Some rides are scary, some are exciting, some are breathtaking and wondrous, and all the while my unseen Lover is right there with His arms wrapped firmly around me. It's interesting how learning to exercise trust in Him is not just having effects on my levels of peace, comfort and assurance as I learn to enter into them in various situations, but also how it seems to be affecting my personality. I can't treat God with the same no-nonsense, ultra-efficient, get-things-done behaviours and attitudes. Surrender and submission produce such opposite feelings and ways of expressing myself. Efficiency and getting stuff done are traits God clearly has no intentions of removing from me, thanks to how He seems to keep taking me into situations needing them. But He's softening me. . . I'm losing my edge!

A Gift

Would you believe that while I hadn't expected Christmas music so soon in the Fall of 2007, that "Drummer Boy" the traditional boys choir version, brought me to tears at lunch one day? We all know the lyrics. It was as if I saw myself as that little boy, with my skills and talents being all I could offer seeming so small in light of the majesty, power, and greatness of the One before me, meekly asking if it's OK if I share what little I have and upon finding it accepted, at the line where Mary nods to the young lad, I began to cry. That song used to touch me before, but not like this.

Sometimes I think this heart isn't just softening, it's turning to mush! It doesn't take much to get me teary-eyed these days at all. Music is such a powerful medium over which the truths of God's Word and the longings of His heart can travel. This author sings in the choir, subbed on praise teams, and has Praise106.5 going on the computer and a CD of choir songs and worship choruses in the car! I have discovered that if you go into choir songs with the right attitude, with the right spirit, that even Christmas can be a time of worship! This is indeed a pleasant soft light bulb this year.

Relationship. . . that desire I entered the Christmas season of 2007 with. . . is something God wants with us. . . The manger is empty now. . . The cross is empty. . . The crown is yet to be donned in preparation for that trip back to earth riding a white horse! The baby has grown and become the Bridegroom. . . and it seems. . . to me anyway. . . that now He wants to celebrate His birthday with those longing to be of His Bride. . . Couples like to greet each other with a hug and a kiss on their special day. . . So why wouldn't the celestial Birthday Boy not seek a little affection from His Bride on His birthday?! He wants relationship with us. . . The songs that were chosen for Christmas that year, and how God wanted to use the themes that Christmas all speak to God's desire for restored relationship with mankind. . . God coming down to man. . . Emmanuel. . .

> **Isaiah 9:6** For unto us a child is born, unto us a son is given: and the government shall be upon his shoulder: and his name shall be called Wonderful, Counsellor, The mighty God, The everlasting Father, The Prince of Peace.

Beth Moore capped off one study, being asked if she really believed in the whole Prince Charming riding in on a white horse to sweep her off her feet and ride off into the sunset. . . She replied quoting the passage in **Revelation 19:11-16** where indeed Christ does return dressed in white, riding a white horse, with His Crown on His head and a sword in His hand. Imagine thinking of Christ as Prince Charming. . . but don't we sing of Him being our Prince of Peace? Isn't that a title given to Him from Scripture? Indeed He is the One and Only Prince Charming that will ever grace this planet! He wants relationship!!!

I get the feeling He's tired of us just flipping through the eternal photo album, smiling at His baby pictures and cooing over them like we do every year. He wants us looking at Him! He wants to take us in His arms and remind us of why He really came! He's hoping to have a grown-up celebration this year! He wants to take His Bride in His arms, listen to her wish Him another Happy Birthday, gaze into her eyes, whisper again what He thinks of her, why He came, and hold her as she melts into a puddle of gratitude against His chest, totally filled with awe, appreciation, gratefulness and love for all He came to do.

Christmas really does feel so much more intimate. My eyes were moist at various times, from singing "Shine on Us", to "Light a Candle"...

To view lyrics for songs referenced in this chapter,
please visit http://songdove.fa-ct.com/
There you will find interactive Scripture references, videos containing lyrics to most of the songs listed here, topics mentioned in this chapter, and more.

Scriptures used, referred to or that relate to thoughts in this session:

Revelation 19:11-16   Isaiah 9:6

Songs shared, referenced, or that relate to thoughts in this session:

Drummer Boy   Light a Candle
Shine on Us

Topics discussed, referred to, or that relate to thoughts in this session:

Relationship with God and mankind   Christmas
(No physical contact)   Prince of Peace
God's Agape Love   Softening

Questions for Discussion:

What does Christmas mean to you personally? Be honest.

_____

_____

Have you ever considered Christmas in the manner introduced here?

_____

_____

How is Christ described in Isaiah 9:6?

_____

_____

How will Christ return according to Revelation 19:11-16?

_____

_____

Does Prince Charming exist? _____

_____

Little Drummer Boy: Lyrics

Come they told me, pa rum pum pum pum
A new born King to see, pa rum pum pum pum
Our finest gifts we bring, pa rum pum pum pum
To lay before the King, pa rum pum pum pum,
rum pum pum pum, rum pum pum pum,

So to honour Him, pa rum pum pum pum,
When we come.

Little Baby,
pa rum pum pum pum
I am a poor boy too, pa rum pum pum pum
I have no gift to bring, pa rum pum pum pum
That's fit to give the King, pa rum pum pum pum,
rum pum pum pum, rum pum pum pum,

Shall I play for you, pa rum pum pum pum,
On my drum?

Mary nodded, pa rum pum pum pum
The ox and lamb kept time, pa rum pum pum pum
I played my drum for Him, pa rum pum pum pum
I played my best for Him, pa rum pum pum pum,
rum pum pum pum, rum pum pum pum,

Then He smiled at me, pa rum pum pum pum
Me and my drum.

Public Domain

Shine On Us
CCLI Song No. 1754646
© 1996 Sony/ATV Milene Music | Deer Valley Music | (Admin. by Sony/ATV Milene Music)
Deborah D. Smith | Michael W. Smith

Light A Candle
CCLI Song No. 3067918
© 2000 Christian Taylor Music | Paragon Music Corporation | Vacation Boy Music (Admin. by Integrated Copyright Group, Inc.) | (Admin. by Brentwood-Benson Music Publishing, Inc.) | (Admin. by Brentwood-Benson Music Publishing, Inc., 741 Cool Springs Blvd., Franklin TN 37067)
Joel Lindsey | Wayne Haun

Binding up Our Wounds

> **Psalm 147:3** He healeth the broken in heart, and bindeth up
> their wounds.

All of a sudden one day, I became aware of why I've seen so many changes
since March of 2007! Beth was talking about how we need to let God bind
up our wounds, and definitions like bind, wrap around, envelope, enclose
were being used, and a light bulb went on in my head. I've been talking about
how God seems to wrap me in enveloping hugs, completely surrounding me
in such warm intimacy as if I could almost touch Him. . . and while I've been
experiencing these displays, Grandma and others have been talking about
watching me change. Grandma says she's been seeing me mature before her
eyes, as if something was keeping me back in that aspect of developing as a
person spiritually. . . Suddenly I understood why those changes were happening, where this softening has been coming from, and why life doesn't seem so
raw anymore. . . God's act of wrapping Himself around me has been to bind
up the wounds I've suffered over the years. . . Is it any wonder I never want
those moments to end??? Why I wish I could stay in those hugs ALL the
time??? All I could do was sit there mentally going "wow. . .oh wow. . ."

Beth Moore mentioned at the end of the video series, that God wanted to
speak to someone who had thought God could never use them again, or
never use them to the level at which He'd done before they fell. She said that
was a lie, and that this video would end with a prayer of dedication, or re-ded-
ication for those that needed it. She said that in spite of whatever it was that
we felt was holding us back, or that we thought would stop God's hand in our
lives, that God's hand was not stopped, and that God desired that we no
longer be held back. There are so many times when I feel this way it's not
funny. But knowing and watching God's restoring hand since my divorce,
slow at first, but drastically picking up steam, has been so healing! The restoration has not just been in the realm of service and giftings, but of my own
sense of wellbeing, my own sense of usability, of still being worth something
to the service of the Kingdom.

To read Scriptures referenced in this chapter,
please visit http://songdove.fa-ct.com/
There you will find interactive Scripture references, videos containing lyrics to
most of the songs in these chapters, topics mentioned in this chapter, and
more.

Scriptures used, referred to or that relate to thoughts in this session:

Psalm 147:3

Topics discussed, referred to, or that relate to thoughts in this session:

Healing   Restoring
Binding up wounds

Questions for Discussion:

Are there wounds in your life God wants to bind up and heal?

_____

_____

What have you been held back from in your own mind because of wounds in
your past?

_____

_____

What is required to receive God's healing in this area?

_____

_____

Amazing love

I surrender. . . that phrase started circulating in my head. . . my heart is bowing as it runs through my mind. . . as if to back this up, "Amazing love" by Billy Foote, just came on the radio!

He loves me in spite of irrational moments, reminding me of His love, of His sacrifice, of how much I mean to Him. . . declaration after declaration of all that Christ did for me. . . for the shame of the choices I made. . . He tells me that He forgave me, that He died for these sins, to just leave them there, to refocus on Him instead of on how far I fell. I want to cling to these lyrics. . . to these reminders. . . as the song carries on, "in all I do, I honour You". . . I do wish to honour my Lord in all I do. . . that's why learning to show God's agape love has meant so much to me.

I had no idea passing through the Fruit of the Spirit on such an intimate level would touch areas that are still healing in my own life. I encountered more ouch moments than I anticipated.

Cracked Pots

My daughter asked me to tell her about the small banner I now have over my monitor "The Water of Life Flows Through Broken Vessels", so I told her one Sunday night, the "Tale of Two Pots" and found myself choking up and getting misty-eyed as I shared what this story meant to me. She went away with some deep thoughts of her own. Let me share one of its many renditions here: You can find a tear-out of this small banner at the end of this chapter.

"A Tale of Two Pots"

A water bearer had two large pots, each hung on each end of a pole which he carried across his neck.

One of the pots had a crack in it, and while the other pot was perfect and always delivered a full portion of water at the end of the long walk from the stream to the master's house, the cracked pot arrived only half full.

For a full two years this went on daily, with the bearer delivering only one and a half pots full of water in his master's house.

Of course, the perfect pot was proud of its accomplishments, perfect to the end for which it was made.

But the poor cracked pot was ashamed of its own imperfection, and miserable that it was able to accomplish only half of what it had been made to do.

After two years of what it perceived to be a bitter failure, it spoke to the water bearer one day by the stream.

"I am ashamed of myself, and I want to apologize to you."
"Why?" asked the bearer. "What are you ashamed of?"

"I have been able, for these past two years, to deliver only half my load because this crack in my side causes water to leak out all the way back to your master's house. Because of my flaws, you have to do all of this work, and you don't get full value from your efforts," the pot said.

The water bearer felt sorry for the old cracked pot, and in his compassion he said, "As we return to the master's house, I want you to notice the beautiful flowers along the path."

Indeed as they went up the hill, the old cracked pot took notice of the sun warming the beautiful wild flowers on the side of the path and this cheered it some. But at the end of the trail, it still felt bad because it had leaked out half its load, and so again it apologized to the bearer for its failure.

The bearer said to the pot, "Did you notice that there were flowers only on your side of your path, but not on the other pot's side? That's because I have always known about your flaw, and I took advantage of it. I planted flower seeds on your side of the path, and every day while we walk back from the stream, you've watered them.

For two years, I have been able to pick these beautiful flowers to decorate my master's table. Without you being just the way you are, he would not have this beauty to grace his house."
***

Marble

God's love for me is bringing me to that place of accepting the cracks in my life. One time I heard someone talk about marble, how its beauty comes from the random lines, thin and thick that run through it, and how our lives are like that marble, with scars thin and thick running through it contributing to the beauty of who God is shaping us to be. One could say God's Temple is paved with living marble. . . different shades and colours with varying degrees of scarred lines. . .

> **Isaiah 61:3** To appoint unto them that mourn in Zion, to give unto them beauty for ashes, the oil of joy for mourning, the garment of praise for the spirit of heaviness; that they might be called trees of righteousness, the planting of the LORD, that he might be glorified.

Beauty for ashes, a trail of flowers where the water of life seeps out of the cracks of a yielded broken vessel. . . God's arms of love feel as if they are wrapped around this heart as I type this. . . I sense such warmth and healing as I let these thoughts roll around my heart and mind. . . I am not a lost cause.

I may not understand the unlimited unfathomable depth of God's love for me in all its unconditional intimacy and passion. . . but I wish to surrender to it, to submit to it, to let it flow over me in all its healing restoring comforting power. . .

So much going on in life. . . so much going on in this heart. . . One song on Praise106.5, Seasons of Love by Chris Faulk, calls Christmas the season of love. . . drawing us into the Throne Room of the King of Kings, the One who truly wishes to take us onto His lap, holding us close to His chest, embracing us, holding us, and seeking to heal, to restore, to grant us our needs, and those requests that echo the desires of His heart.

The car was playing "Kindness" again as I drove to get my daughter from the barn before work one morning and I couldn't help almost swooning as I admitted once more that yes, indeed it is God's incredible kindness and love for me that brings me to that place of repentance, of willing brokenness before Him. His love somehow breaks through the toughest shell. This Brazil nut has had her shell breached and broken open, and yet without scattering me to the wind doing so.

Somehow God used my pastor to soften this shell, and while I am still feeling the sometimes raw tenderness of exposure, God is right there wrapping me up with His love at the exact same time, and others are right there with their continued encouragement and care. Amazingly, while I am feeling more spiritually/relationally exposed to the unseen elements, the sense of protection is far easier to recognize and accept than it was while I was whipped around in my storm desperately trying to open up while keeping my shell wrapped tightly around me.

I can't keep that shell wrapped up anymore. Ever since the beginning of March 2007, God has been peeling it away. I can feel the tenderizing effects too. The way I think has been really affected!!! I'm still falling into old ways occasionally. Christmas evening that year at dinner, Isaiah commented on behaviour that he said I engage in that I was telling him we need to try to avoid. He was being very selfish about what he did and didn't want to put up with in a way that didn't show much care for those going through or exhibiting the things that bugged him. I realized at that moment that my thoughts really have changed and I felt corrected in my spirit that how I'd been living and behaving in front of my kids was now being seen as unhealthy, and I couldn't help agreeing that it was. God directly, through others and the teaching I am sitting under has all been showing me the answer to my question, how to show God's love to those around me! I stand convicted of some of my behaviour for sure!

I was sharing some of this with a friend one night, and she confirmed that even she's seen changes in me since she arrived a year before. While it makes me uncomfortable to hear, having that assurance from someone else that these changes aren't "all in my head" is comforting. But changing my thinking and softening my feelings has been something God's been very actively doing. The challenge is always in the working out of those things. But with conviction of less than loving behaviour toward others coming so much more frequently now, I'm hoping that the working out will be easier for me to see in the future. Where "the rubber meets the road" is always where the skinned knees and stubbed noses come from. I pray I don't skin my knees too often as I learn how to put the Fruit of the Spirit into action.

I've never had Christmas work itself into an ongoing teaching like that! But this one year it sure did! I've touched on a few of the attributes that I've seen in how God used Christ's birth as a display of His love toward mankind, but I'm sure if I looked deeper, I'd see all 9 Fruit of the Spirit in that event over 2000 years ago! These lessons and revelations truly did not stop over Christmas but continue to this day!

To view lyrics for songs referenced in this chapter,
please visit http://songdove.fa-ct.com/
There you will find interactive Scripture references, videos containing lyrics to most of the songs listed here, topics mentioned in this chapter, and more.

Scriptures used, referred to or that relate to thoughts in this session:

Isaiah 61   Galatians 5:22-23

Songs shared, referenced, or that relate to thoughts in this session:

Amazing love   Kindness
Season of Love

Topics discussed, referred to, or that relate to thoughts in this session:

Relationship with God and mankind   Christmas
(No physical contact)   Prince of Peace
God's Agape Love   Softening

Questions for Discussion:

Fun Question: I liken myself to being a Brazil nut. If you had to describe yourself as a Christmas nut, which one would you be and why?

_____

_____

How does God soften our hearts? _____

_____

Are there ashes in your life? What beauty has God pulled from them?

_____

_____

Using the topical search on the website, or the nearest Strong's Concordance, find the verse that speaks of being built up as living stones in the Temple of God and quote it here:

_____

_____

You Are My King (Amazing Love)

CCLI Song No. 2456623

© 1996 worshiptogether.com songs (Admin. by EMI Christian Music Publishing)

Billy Foote

Season Of Love

CCLI Song No. 3406940

© 2001 Pelican Lips Music | Jax & Broder Music | Topboost Music | Deston Songs | Boat Money Music (Admin. by ION Music Administration) | (Admin. by ION Music Administration, LLC) | (Admin. by Moon & Musky Music) | | Chris Faulk | George Cocchini | Hunter Davis

Kindness

CCLI Song No. 3028373

© 2000 worshiptogether.com songs | sixsteps Music (Admin. by EMI Christian Music Publishing) | (Admin. by EMI Christian Music Publishing)

Chris Tomlin | Jesse Reeves | Louie Giglio

The Water of Life flows
through broken vessels

Of Snakes and Hay Fever

It continues to amaze me that God knows what I need to hear long before I realize I need it, many times actually stating it through my own pen and fingers before I fully realize what I've shared. God allowed me to use my favourite reptile to express what I'd read once described in a rose and lily. My reader will find this story in a chapter later in this book.

I actually prefer the image of a warm cozy snake curled up on His chest as opposed to something that causes me hay fever, but God seems to like the image of a flower Himself. Snakes like to go where it's warm, and their little faces are so expressive when they are restful, cozy, cold, or warm. Their little muscles relax too when they are warm and restful. A peaceful sleeping snake just makes me go "awwwwww". They are sooo cute! And they respond to warm gentle touch too.

A rose wilts after awhile, dries up and blows away after being plucked from the plant it grew on. Doesn't sound very appealing to me. An author who shared this could have adjusted that analogy by having the King plant the rose in His own garden, using the analogy of Christ as the vine and we as the branches. In such a case the rose would always open up to the Sun of the Morning, always welcome the warmth of His love and never wilt, dry up and blow away, but always waft its fragrance in deepest gratitude to the One that nurtured it so lovingly, so tenderly, so unconditionally. I think I prefer that description a lot more personally. I'm glad God doesn't have hay fever.

Bruised Petals

The relational preparation its felt as if I've been undergoing, that was referenced a few times over the late spring and into the summer months during that first eventful year of this journey, has been confirmed to be happening and still directed at my Lord. A friend feels God is taking me in His hands the way my husband was supposed to have, and is using others to draw me to Himself in ways that are not only restorative, but opening me as a flower opens to the warmth of the sun. . . The bruised petals open slower and more hesitantly than the healthy ones, but this is why I get to overflowing with gratitude at the efforts of those God has brought into my life!

> **Isaiah 43:18-19** Remember ye not the former things, neither consider the things of old. [19]Behold, I will do a new thing; now it shall spring forth; shall ye not know it? I will even make a way in the wilderness, and rivers in the desert.

I can't help wondering if that's going to be this whole concept of sharing with others what God is teaching me about learning to live as the Bride of Christ in a fallen world. It is apparent from a quick glance through history, that God has sought to teach people about this at various times through the centuries, evident in biographical writings, hymns that were penned. Even in a half-hour video I sent everyone on Facebook, people were talking about the holiness and judgement of a good and loving God and how He longs for His Church to be so in love with Him that His people will do anything for Him, how He longs for His Bride to rise up and be the witness she is to be in this world.

Revelation 22:17, And the Spirit and Bride say Come

That reminds me of the last few verses of Revelation. . . The Bride has a role to play, and the Church has largely been lost on that role because of how many centuries we've spent infighting among denominational lines, claiming one is the only way and the rest are going to hell, pointing fingers and trying to trip each other up over doctrinal differences. God is calling to His Bride and it is so exciting for me to hear of others also hearing this call and desiring to respond to it!!!

To read Scriptures referenced in this chapter,
please visit http://songdove.fa-ct.com/
There you will find interactive Scripture references, videos containing lyrics to most of the songs in these chapters, topics mentioned in this chapter, and more.

Scriptures used, referred to or that relate to thoughts in this session:

Isaiah 43:18-19   Revelation 22:17

Topics discussed, referred to, or that relate to thoughts in this session:

Bride of Christ   Flower petals
Bridegroom   Transformation

Questions for Discussion:

Who is the Bride of Christ?

_____

_____

Look up " bruised reed" in the topical search for chapter 3 on the website or
the nearest Strong's Concordance. What verse does it come from and what
does that verse say about God's character?

_____

_____

Butterflies

I have felt like a flower in the hand of my mentor as he's done so much to encourage, steady, constrain and restore me to the giftings, talents, skills and abilities God wants to revive in my ministerial life. Now the image of the butterfly has been given to me in tangible form. First on the gift box by a friend, then on a velvet coloured poster my daughter bought from the Michael's craft store, then on my daughter's new worship flags. Sometimes I feel like I can identify more with the flower than with the butterfly, feeling like some of the petals are damaged, but healing under the gentle caring touch of my mentor, and encouraged to open by God's influence through him and others around me. But the ladies prayer group I was part of, sees me as a butterfly coming forth and learning to stretch my wings and that one day I will have them stretched wide open for all to enjoy.

Musings

In the chronological way these notes have been written, February 2008 has started. . . the so-called "love" month. . . This year I found something I didn't have the previous 8 years. . . the introduction of God as my unseen Lover, my unseen Husband. I don't know if He thinks how we tend to celebrate this month is worth emulating or not, but we'll find out. He doesn't need Valentines to express His love for us. "Here with me" began to play on Praise106.5 by MercyMe as I first penned these thoughts. Such an intimate song!!! But one evening as I was sitting on the couch, I was enveloped yet again, He felt so intimately close, and it did feel in my heart and spirit, that I was being held. God is so amazingly personal, yet so all powerful. I don't know if I'll ever get over that contrast!

To think. . . to experience the arms of my God, the arms of One who made the Universe, the arms of One who has judged entire nations, the One who died to save me, who died so that I would not be lost to hell but rescued to join Him at His side for all eternity. . . Talk about the ultimate rags to riches story, the ultimate beggar to Queen transformation. . .

Isaiah 62:5 For as a young man marrieth a virgin, so shall thy sons marry thee: and as the bridegroom rejoiceth over the bride, so shall thy God rejoice over thee.

The Bride of Christ will one day become the true Queen of Heaven as Christ rules for all eternity and the Bride stands at His side to rule and reign with Him!!! It isn't Mary all by herself as is so blasphemously stated by those who would perpetrate Dianna worship in the church! She will simply be one of many who have embraced Christ as their own down through the ages! All of us forming the Body of Christ, dressed in the robes of Righteousness He's given us, each with our abilities and giftings given us by Christ Himself, by the Holy Spirit, and crowned with the Crown of Life. What a picture, what an amazing picture!

To view lyrics for songs referenced in this chapter,
please visit http://songdove.fa-ct.com/
There you will find interactive Scripture references, videos containing lyrics to most of the songs listed here, topics mentioned in this chapter, and more.

Scriptures used, referred to or that relate to thoughts in this session:

Isaiah 62:5

Songs shared, referenced, or that relate to thoughts in this session:

Here With Me

Topics discussed, referred to, or that relate to thoughts in this session:

Bride of Christ	Transformation
Bridegroom	Preparation
Butterflies	

Questions for Discussion:

Are you going through a transformation? How would you describe it?

_____

_____

Care to share any stories of God's restoration in your life?

_____

_____

Here With Me
CCLI Song No. 4312143
© 2004 Simpleville Music | Songs From The Indigo Room | Wordspring Music, LLC | Wet As A Fish Music | Zooki Tunes | Russell Made Music (Admin. by Simpleville Music, Inc.) | (Admin. by Word Music Group, Inc.) | (Admin. by Word Music Group, Inc.) | (Admin. by Simpleville Music, Inc.) | (Admin. by Word Music Group, Inc.) | (Admin. by Fun Attic Music) Barry Graul | Bart Millard | Brad Russell | Dan Muckala | Jim Bryson | Mike Scheuchzer | Nathan Cochran | Peter Kipley | Robby Shaffer

God's Choosing

> **Job 11:6** And that he would shew thee the secrets of wisdom, that they are double to that which is! Know therefore that God exacteth of thee less than thine iniquity deserveth.

Someone told me it seems I've helped a lot of people. . . That's part of what amazes me about how God has used me in years past. I guess it's safe to say that He uses us at the understanding level we are at, at whatever stage of faith we are at regardless of the stage of life we are at. Because if God's use of this vessel were dependent on the perfect life, I would never have touched the lives I've touched. When I look back at myself in those years, it truly does blow me away that God saw fit to use this obviously broken vessel. I just didn't know how broken I was. Now that I do, I look at myself and I know if it had been me, I wouldn't have chosen me for things God did. But God chose me anyway. It's like Job's ordeal, when his so-called friends were "counselling" him. God has not treated me according to my sin, according to my mistakes, according to my humanity, but instead has chosen to treat me according to who He sees me to be in Christ!

> **1 Corinthians 1:26-31** For ye see your calling, brethren, how that not many wise men after the flesh, not many mighty, not many noble, are called: ²⁷But God hath chosen the foolish things of the world to confound the wise; and God hath chosen the weak things of the world to confound the things which are mighty; ²⁸And base things of the world, and things which are despised, hath God chosen, yea, and things which are not, to bring to nought things that are: ²⁹That no flesh should glory in his presence. ³⁰But of him are ye in Christ Jesus, who of God is made unto us wisdom, and righteousness, and sanctification, and redemption: ³¹That, according as it is written, He that glorieth, let him glory in the Lord.

Talk about a humbling thought! His Word says He takes the foolish things of this world to confound the wise. . . *shakes head* no kidding. . . The ministerial resume built up from that of a child till now can read like a lot of accomplishments minus bible college, but there is no way anymore I can look on that list with any sort of pride, just amazement. Truly God does take us at whatever state we are at, takes the willing heart toward serving in His Kingdom, and uses us for His glory, not our own.

There were times in my faith walk where I indeed lived the squeaky-clean life, but there were other times when I was in rebellion against my Dad, angry, and those led to choices that eventually got me to where I am today. But interspersed through it all God led me across various people's paths, and God chose to touch those people through me.

There is a sense of comfort in the knowledge that God didn't put me on a shelf because of my poor choices in life. I suppose it helps that none of my poor choices resulted in all-out deliberate sin either, as we know that God will not use the heart that wilfully engages in known sin until after that person repents. God gives guidelines in Scripture for disciplining such believers in the hopes they will repent of their sin and turn back onto the right path. I am thankful that God kept me through the times when I could have engaged in known sin. Yet another point of thankfulness and gratitude toward His Hand in my life.

I can't take personal credit for the lives God has touched through me. I just praise God that He saw fit to use me in their lives for good and not detriment. The more I learn of God's intimate love for me, the more I realize that it is through no status or accomplishment of my own that God sees fit to use me, but that it is entirely of His choosing, His timing, and His enabling that I have accomplished anything for the Kingdom of God. I am so filled with gratitude for how He has seen fit to use me, gifted me, etc. It behooves me to remember where these abilities and opportunities come from, and for whom they are aimed.

1 Corinthians 12:7-11 But the manifestation of the Spirit is given to every man to profit withal. ⁸For to one is given by the Spirit the word of wisdom; to another the word of knowledge by the same Spirit; ⁹To another faith by the same Spirit; to another the gifts of healing by the same Spirit; ¹⁰To another the working of miracles; to another prophecy; to another discerning of spirits; to another divers kinds of tongues; to another the interpretation of tongues: ¹¹But all these worketh that one and the selfsame Spirit, dividing to every man severally as he will.

God gifts and equips us with talents and abilities, skills and bents in life that are meant to be somehow used to further the Kingdom of God. Whether through equipping the saints, pushing open the doors of the Inner Court in worship, doing battle in prayer, or reaching the lost on the front lines, we each have a part to play in the Kingdom of God and have been granted what we need to fulfill our roles. God's Word also says that when we need something He will provide it, that the Holy Spirit gives out Gifts as He deems fit, so as we need a particular gifting, He will provide it at the time required. We can't take any credit for what God has and continues to do through us. All glory goes back to Him and Him alone.

To read Scriptures referenced in this chapter,
please visit http://songdove.fa-ct.com/
There you will find interactive Scripture references, videos containing lyrics to most of the songs in these chapters, topics mentioned in this chapter, and more.

Scriptures used, referred to or that relate to thoughts in this session:

Job 11:6   1 Corinthians 12:7-11
1 Corinthians 1:26-31

Topics discussed, referred to, or that relate to thoughts in this session:

Chosen   Man's versus God's choosing
Giftings   Holy Spirit giftings

Questions for Discussion:

Who chooses us for service? Why? _____

_____

Who takes credit for what we do in God's name? Why?

_____

_____

Are you glad God doesn't wait till we're perfect before using us in His King-dom? Why or why not?

_____

_____

In a Land, Far, Far away. . . But Closer than Any of Us Realize. . . the Following Story Continued. . .

The Crown Prince noticed lacerations peeking out from under the tattered sleeve of her dress. He was about to ask permission to heal them when she caught his gaze and quickly covered them up!

"My Lady," He began softly, "If you will let me, I can heal those too. . ."

She opened her mouth to answer just as rocks began to land around them. The Crown Prince jumped to his feet, observing with one sweep of his eyes that the townsfolk had come out of the city pelting rocks at them! Sensing the danger, Swift Wind quickly advanced and the Prince swung the young lady onto the horse before climbing on himself. Quickly he spun the horse around and galloped out of sight.

Now the young lady was quite puzzled as to who this man was. As they rode along, she tried to put the pieces of her day together. Was she dreaming? Could this really be happening? Why would a complete stranger do all these things for her?

"Maria you are worth too much to let them kill you back there."

Startled, she straightened up, "You know my name? How is it you know my name?"

"I know the names of all my countrymen, Maria." Finally a good distance away from town, the Crown Prince spotted a spring in the distance. "Let us head for that spring and relax for a bit."

Dismounting both himself and the young lady, he walked Swift Wind to the edge of the pool and sat down to rest. Maria walked to its edge, and after satiating her thirst, turned to the Crown Prince.

"Who are you, and what do you want with me?!"

The Crown Prince smiled as he played with a stick in the grass. "You honestly don't know who has rescued you. . ." Maria shook her head. "Maria, I am the Crown Prince, I gave you that robe when you first accepted my offer of salvation from the dark ones."

Maria's jaw dropped! Suddenly she was even more ashamed of her state, and especially of the once beautiful robe that hung stained and torn around her. Tears began to fall as she replied, "But my Prince, can you not see how I have soiled your robe? I am not fit for your Kingdom, least of all for your attention to my wounds."

At this the Crown Prince got up and walked over to her with the kindest, warmest, most disarming eyes she'd ever seen. "Maria, I died for you, and now I have chosen you as my Bride. I love you more than any peasant male ever will and I long to make you whole again and present you to my Father. There is only one thing I ask of you."

Maria's face fell even more as she wiped a tear from her cheek.

"All I ask is that you surrender to my touch. Let me see every part of your body that has been harmed and let me heal it. Let me mend your robe and make it new again. It may mean some changes in how you look after yourself, perhaps changes in how you interact with fellow peasants on the road or in town, but please. . . Let me do this. Let me make you whole again."

Maria sank into the grass realizing the weight of the Crown Prince's request. The thought of being whole appealed to her, but His request meant that she had to let Him into every area of her life! Her head dropped into her hands as she struggled and fought between receiving healing and becoming vulnerable.

When she looked up again, Swift Wind was resting on the ground near a tree. The Crown Prince was standing in front of her with his arms outstretched. Once again she saw the purest and deepest love she'd ever seen in His eyes. She stood up, reached out for his hands, lowered her head and nodded. Her shaking form showed the Prince just how scared she was of the coming period of healing and restoration, but her submission to His hand made Him smile. He gathered her to Himself and held her close for awhile.

* * *

Surrender to the Holy Spirit. . .

By now you've discovered that this book is a very personal trip into the heart of a very personal God. The previous chapter introduced the reader to a number of concepts that will get fleshed out in greater detail as we progress. In this chapter, I will take you through some of the challenges and revelations, lessons and discoveries as God began teaching me what happens when a person truly does surrender their life to Christ! As you go through this and subsequent chapters in this book, you may discover areas in your own life where God has been issuing you challenges, wanting to teach you things and asking for your surrender. I would urge you as these things come to mind, write them down. Perhaps write them in the sidebar of this book, along with the date when you realize God is speaking to you on that issue. In this way we may journey together into the intimate heart of God.

I need to start out by saying that God really does want to be included in our lives! Scripture is so full of His desire to be there when times are tough, to be there when times are good, to be our strength in a very real and immediate way!

God's Grace offered in our Struggles

One night I was making a journal entry to God about my desire to be wrapped up in arms of comfort and security. His rather powerful reply emphasized that what I long for is found through surrender to the Holy Spirit's infilling in my life. Again, musical lyrics struck! Song verses that spoke of God's mercy in a hymn I'd never heard before, "He Giveth More Grace" by Annie J. Flint, spoke of His grace, of His sustaining and restoring power through the storms of life. That hymn felt as if it had been written just for me!

A verse entered my mind containing the phrase, "deep calls unto deep at the voice of thy waterspouts". I shared with a friend how God's been touching me and I said, "you know what waterspouts are don't you? Underwater volcanoes???"

This friend turned around and said "You have had a few of those have you not?" All I could answer was a quick, firm "uh-huh, yup!" Well, I located the chapter this verse is found in, in the book of Psalm. David could have written it about me with a few minor details changed here and there, and perhaps it might echo your own heart?

> **Psalms 42:1-7** To the chief Musician, Maschil, for the sons of Korah. As the hart panteth after the water brooks, so panteth my soul after thee, O God. ²My soul thirsteth for God, for the living God: when shall I come and appear before God? ³My tears have been my meat day and night, while they continually say unto me, Where is thy God? ⁴When I remember these things, I pour out my soul in me: for I had gone with the multitude, I went with them to the house of God, with the voice of joy and praise, with a multitude that kept holyday. ⁵Why art thou cast down, O my soul? and why art thou disquieted in me? hope thou in God: for I shall yet praise him for the help of his countenance. ⁶O my God, my soul is cast down within me: therefore will I remember thee from the land of Jordan, and of the Hermonites, from the hill Mizar. ⁷Deep calleth unto deep at the noise of thy waterspouts: all thy waves and thy billows are gone over me. *(the waterspouts many of which happened in the fall of 2006 before my breakthrough in 2007 and some of which came afterward)* ⁸Yet the LORD will command his lovingkindness in the daytime, and in the night his song shall be with me, and my prayer unto the God of my life. ⁹I will say unto God my rock, Why hast thou forgotten me? why go I mourning because of the oppression of the enemy? ¹⁰As with a sword in my bones, mine enemies reproach me; while they say daily unto me, Where is thy God? ¹¹Why art thou cast down, O my soul? and why art thou disquieted within me? hope thou in God: for I shall yet praise him, who is the health of my countenance, and my God.

This is one of those Psalms where I echo so much of what the Psalmist writes. . . The awesome thing is that as deeply as I long to be found in my Lord's presence, He longs for it even more and shows up every time I choose to quiet my spirit and draw near, whether at home or in His House, or amazingly enough at times, in my car.

To view lyrics for songs referenced in this chapter,
please visit http://songdove.fa-ct.com/
There you will find interactive Scripture references, videos containing lyrics to most of the songs listed here, topics mentioned in this chapter, and more.

Scriptures used, referred to or that relate to thoughts in this session:

Psalm 42: 1 – 11

Songs shared, referenced, or that relate to thoughts in this session:

He Giveth More Grace

Topics discussed, referred to, or that relate to thoughts in this session:

Offering self as an act of worship   Broken – independent spirit
Submission/Trust   Brokenness
Trust – surrender   Letting God live through us
Trust-peace-rest   Remain open during trials and tests
Obedience, humbleness, surrender

Questions for Discussion:

Can you recall a stormy time in your life?_ _____

_____

What verse in Psalm 42 stood out to you? _____

_____

Listen to the hymn mentioned in this devotional (on the website). How do the words of this hymn reflect the thoughts in Psalm 42?

_____

_____

He Giveth More Grace

CCLI Song No. 14466
© 1941. Renewed 1969 Lillenas Publishing Company | Lillenas Publishing Company | (Admin(s): Music Services, Inc.)
Annie Johnson Flint | Hubert Mitchel

WARNING: Worshipper at the wheel! Watch for random slowdowns!"

One morning as I was driving out to a farm, "Amazed" came on in the car. I found myself getting into the song as I rounded a corner by the hay field when I realized I was blissfully slowing down!!! I was like "Aaaaaaaa, this song is lulling me and I'm driving!!!". I quickly got back up to speed, but wow. . . I knew that song touched me, but didn't realize it would produce such a quieting within me that it would relax even my physical body as my foot eased off the gas pedal. Almost makes me want to create a bumper sticker that says "WARNING: Worshipper at the wheel! Watch for random slowdowns!"

I simply can't get enough of being wrapped in God's presence, wrapped in His embrace and just spending time together. Sometimes it feels that I might fall asleep in those moments. But as much as I long for and engage God in those times, as much as I eagerly look forward to those corporate moments in His presence right along with the Psalmist in Psalm 42, there are also those times when like the Psalmist, my own soul can be cast down, melancholy, even downright depressed. It is in those times when like the Psalmist, I choose to praise the Lord, I choose to worship Him. . .

> **Psalm 42:5** Why art thou cast down, O my soul? and why art thou disquieted in me? hope thou in God: for I shall yet praise him for the help of his countenance.

The Psalmist puts it so well, going on to say why his soul is cast down within him, the struggles he's facing at the moment in time when he penned this psalm. The depths of his soul cry out to God, "deep calleth unto deep at the noise of thy waterspouts". But even in the middle of his struggle, he remembers something in **verse 8,**

> **Psalm 42:5** Yet the Lord will command his lovingkindness in the daytime, and in the night his song shall be with me, and my prayer unto the God of my life.

There it is again. Our God sings over us in the night watches. . . God woke me up one morning having merged two songs together. I'd awakened with this song medley playing in my mind and I couldn't help immediately thinking of those verses where it says God sings over us.

". . . and the voice of truth, says this is for my glory and I will testify to love. . . "

Over and over. . . That same morning I woke up feeling like I was wrapped in His embrace. That's a few years ago now, but I simply cannot forget that morning. I remember running to the verse in Zephaniah where it says my God rejoices over me with songs of deliverance, and that He will rest in His love. He rests in His love for me. . .

I am discovering that when wrapped up in one of those hugs, if I do not rush myself and just rest there, that truly resting in God's love for me is the most quieting, comforting, secure-feeling place I may ever know. . . There is no anxiousness there, no tenseness, no worry, nothing but quietness of heart and soul and spirit, of peace that defies the circumstances outside of that little co-coon. I often wish I didn't have to leave that place to deal with the world around me and its cares, concerns and timetables. Christ couldn't stay in that quiet place all the time either, moving out into the hustle and bustle of daily 1st century life in order to touch the lives of those who so desperately needed Him. So it is with us today, those times of intimacy that are so quieting, com-forting, refreshing and restoring must give way to becoming a conduit for that love into the hearts and lives of those out in today's society who need Him so badly.

> **Luke 6:12-17** And it came to pass in those days, that he went out into a mountain to pray, and continued all night in prayer to God. [13]And when it was day, he called unto him his disciples: and of them he chose twelve, whom also he named apostles; [14]Simon, (whom he also named Peter,) and Andrew his brother, James and John, Philip and Bartholomew,

¹⁵Matthew and Thomas, James the son of Alphaeus, and Simon called Zelotes, ¹⁶And Judas the brother of James, and Judas Iscariot, which also was the traitor. ¹⁷And he came down with them, and stood in the plain, and the company of his disciples, and a great multitude of people out of all Judaea and Jerusalem, and from the sea coast of Tyre and Sidon, which came to hear him, and to be healed of their diseases;

So whether alone at home during the day, on my bed at night, or with the corporate body of Christ in attendance at God's House, I have a choice to make like the Psalmist does. I must look at my state of heart and mind, and tell myself that regardless of what is going on, I will praise the Lord, I will enter into His presence, because no matter how I may be feeling, God is a great and awesome God worthy of my praise.

The Psalmist finishes this psalm with a very similar question to verse 5, but his answer is slightly and very significantly different. . . **verse 11b**: "for I shall yet praise him, who is the health of my countenance, and my God." Notice the slight difference here? In verse 5, he says "for the help of his countenance." and verse 11, "who is the health of my countenance." These are important phrases to note, because it is through focusing on God, seeking His face and looking deep into our Saviour's eyes that our own countenance changes. . . When Moses finished his encounter with God, he had to veil his face because it glowed too brightly for the people and they hid from him otherwise. When we have been with God, when we have sought His face and spent time in His presence, the saying that we glow is still true today. It might not be a visible glow, but we recognize the spiritual glow in each other, how it lifts our spirits, refreshes our heart and soul, and brings light back into our eyes. God urges us, calls us, longs for us to draw near to Himself, and says that if we will draw near to Him, He will draw near to us. He keeps that promise too!

I long to be in that Presence. . .

A Prayer:

Lord, I know I can't live the life You've called me to on my own, I need Your strength, Your love, and Your sustenance to get through to accomplish all that You've given me to do. I bow my spirit and heart in reverent submission and acknowledgement of how great You are and how small I am. . . It blows my mind that someone as great as You, (and there is no one else as great as You), would choose to love me so much. . .I am in awe of You Father God. . .I am amazed and quite literally eternally grateful to You Jesus for all that You've done for me. . . no one can touch what You did for me on the Cross.

***

Did you pray that prayer with me? Do you need God's strength, love and sustenance to get through your life? Strap on your seatbelt, get your pen ready, because surrender comes with challenges! Walk with me now as I give you, in roughly chronological fashion, what this began to look like.

To view lyrics for songs referenced in this chapter,
please visit http://songdove.fa-ct.com/
There you will find interactive Scripture references, videos containing lyrics to most of the songs listed here, topics mentioned in this chapter, and more.

Scriptures used, referred to or that relate to thoughts in this session:

Psalm 42: 1 – 11   Exodus 34:29
Luke 6:12-17

Songs shared, referenced, or that relate to thoughts in this session:

Amazed   Voice of Truth
Why art Thou Cast Down?   Testify to Love

Topics discussed, referred to, or that relate to thoughts in this session:

Surrender	Gratitude
Fear/Shame	Provision
Trust – surrender	Obedience, humbleness, surrender
Trust-peace-rest	Remain open during trials and tests

Questions for Discussion:

How does God sing over you? _____

_____

Is it easy, or difficult to heed God's call to "come away"? _____

Why? _____

What happened to Moses after he spent time with God? _____

_____

Does God's love amaze you? _____

Why or why not? _____

_____

I'm Amazed
CCLI Song No. 4780861
© 2005 Carol Joy Music (Admin. by ClearBox Rights, LLC)
Carol Cymbala

"Why art Thou Cast Down?"
Not sure who this is by

Voice Of Truth
CCLI Song No. 4196620
© 2003 Sparrow Song | Primary Wave Brian (Chapman Sp Acct) | My Refuge Music | Sony/ATV Tree Publishing (a div. of EMI Christian Music Publishing) | (Admin. by Wixen Music Publishing, Inc.) | (Admin. by EMI Christian Music Publishing) | (Admin. by Sony/ATV Songs LLC)
Mark Hall | Steven Curtis Chapman

Testify To Love
By Avalon

Struggle #1: Motherhood

It seems God's asking me to do a lot of surrendering these days, but this also seems to be part of that whole bit involving moving further into "God's chamber". This may be part of the whole baring and revealing thing God has asked of me, complete with the dredging/healing combination. Mothering is one of those things where I routinely bury how I feel, push it aside, in fact altogether forget about so that life can go on. Do what I need to do, try to guide the kids to do what they need to do, maintain a schedule, juggle conflicting schedules, etc, but never really address how I feel about it all. One day, I don't remember exactly when it was, a friend decided to tell me about this whole mothering thing and how God had chosen me as my kids' mother and how they'd been planned by God for a purpose.

A Prayer:
Oh Lord, help me get through this coming Sunday. . . help me to come to terms with the role You wanted for me as mother to Ashley and Isaiah. . . God I didn't ask for this role, and every mother's day brings back fresh hurt and resentment at being forced into this role, gifts and platitudes frustrate and sometimes nearly anger me Father. This year the thought of what I may see and hear this Sunday brings the threat of tears. Lord, You are working on this heart more deeply than I've ever known before, and I ask for Your gentle touch on this sore spot within me. . . You wanted me to bare stuff like this. . . and it hurts to do so to be totally honest. . . You want me to let go and release it to Your hands. . . but holding onto this meant holding onto a vision of myself, a dream of who I thought I wanted to be. . . I didn't think I had any dreams for myself left. . . living day to day had all but dashed any thought of what I might want for myself in the future. . . but I see I still hold onto one concept of what I wanted to be, and the anger, frustration and resentment are directly related to that because it was thwarted, not allowed to come into being. . . Oh God, help me surrender in this area too. . .
***

I confess I'm not used to feeling so tender about everything, I had hoped that once the roller coaster between October of 2006 and February of 2007 ended, that I'd go back to the way I usually did things, but obviously God decided through His displays to me and the messages coming my way through various people, that life is not to go back to the way it was. The corner that I rounded in March of 2007 shut the door on how I used to think and feel and how I view things and situations, even how I think about, feel toward and view others around me. In most ways the new space God's taken me into is both restful and adventurous, its new territory and most of the time I rise to such challenges. But I knew stuff would come up after God said He wanted to see all of my heart, including the damaged, scarred and wounded areas of it. I guess motherhood is the first area to be addressed on that score. It is one of the bigger sore spots and one I haven't wanted to let go of, it's been one that I've nursed at least once every year since conceiving my son, but as I felt led to pray above, I'm seeing the selfishness of that. All reasons for nursing that hurt relate to my personal desires for myself being slighted, ignored, shoved aside, etc. One more area to die to self and surrender to God's plan for my life instead. . .

The Potter at Work:

> **Jeremiah 18:1-6** The word which came to Jeremiah from the LORD, saying, [2]Arise, and go down to the potter's house, and there I will cause thee to hear my words. [3]Then I went down to the potter's house, and, behold, he wrought a work on the wheels. [4]And the vessel that he made of clay was marred in the hand of the potter: so he made it again another vessel, as seemed good to the potter to make it. [5]Then the word of the LORD came to me, saying, [6]O house of Israel, cannot I do with you as this potter? saith the LORD. Behold, as the clay is in the potter's hand, so are ye in mine hand, O house of Israel.

> **Romans 9:20-21** Nay but, O man, who art thou that repliest against God? Shall the thing formed say to him that formed it, Why hast thou made me thus? [21]Hath not the potter power over the clay, of the same lump to make one vessel unto honour, and another unto dishonour?

Once again I'm preaching at myself and you get to sit there and look on. I can feel God softening me, like how a person softens a lump of dough or clay, gently, caringly, lovingly plying the substance, and applying pressure gently to lumps discovered in the mass, to break them down and smooth them out into the whole lump, carefully picking out crusted and infected portions so as to purify the mass as He works. Touching the tender areas hurts. But He doesn't touch with the sole purpose of causing pain, He wants to heal those areas and make them whole. It's so hard not to recoil and curl up around the hurt to hide it from Him. . . I've asked trusted friends for prayer support as I try to obey God's invitation to bare the sensitive areas of my life to Him. I knew this wasn't going to be easy. . .

Intimacy and Surrender, a re-occurring theme:

I've noticed how every major time of worship before the Lord carries with it a call to deeper intimacy with Him in my life, typically involving the surrender of something standing in the way of that call. Easter 2007 was doing this, bringing me to the place where I was willing to forgive someone. A woman's conference one weekend was like this with me discovering what was needed to fully enter into God's chamber, actually more like a prelude to what was coming. Now I'm facing yet another form of surrender, this time in my personal view of how I wanted to live life versus the path God wanted me to live.

I do want to walk further into God's chamber, I just didn't anticipate prior to the woman's conference, that it would entail stuff like this.

To read Scriptures referenced in this chapter,
please visit http://songdove.fa-ct.com/
There you will find interactive Scripture references, videos containing lyrics to
most of the songs in these chapters, topics mentioned in this chapter, and
more.

Scriptures used, referred to or that relate to thoughts in this session:

Psalm 51:6   Psalm 73:28
Proverbs 20:27   Jeremiah 30:21
Romans 9:20,21   Hebrews 10:22
Jeremiah 18:1-6

Topics discussed, referred to, or that relate to thoughts in this session:

Challenges: Motherhood   Trust – surrender
Die to self   Trust-peace-rest
Offering self as an act of worship Gratitude
Surrender   Provision
Forgiveness   Obedience, humbleness, surrender
Fear/Shame   Broken – independent spirit
Alabaster box   Brokenness
Submission/Trust   Remain open during trials and tests

Questions for Discussion:

Who is the potter in the verses quoted in this study? _____

Who is the clay in the verses quoted in this study? _____

What would it take for you to truly be clay in God's hands?

_____

_____

_____

An image of the Bride of Christ

Sometimes I see an image of the Bride of Christ, sitting or standing in tattered robes, bruises and scars here and there over her frame. This scene has an image of Christ reaching toward her, longing to take her in His arms, longing for her to uncover those bruises and scars so He can pour the Oil of the Spirit into them to heal them, apply the healing Balm of Gilead to her wounds. As she reveals each area, He touches it and indeed it does heal, but she flinches at some and quickly hides others when the pain of the cleansing gets too much for her. This saddens Christ and He gently seeks to have her uncover those areas again so He can continue the task of bringing healing. While I've heard similar less graphic descriptions of the Bride of Christ standing before her Lord, this is certainly how I feel personally. I shouldn't fear the touch of my Kingly Bridegroom, I shouldn't fear letting my heart be fully exposed to Him, what kind of bride is afraid to reveal herself to her husband? *sigh* One who is ashamed of what must be seen. . .

Remember that alabaster box I wrote about in the previous chapter? That sacrifice of praise? It is there in spite of the rawness showing up on this heart after that conference. While it's painful to go through, the fact God loves me enough to desire my healing is in itself cause for praise, thanksgiving and worship. That He can see the areas I am ashamed of and love me in spite of them is indeed cause for loving Him in return, out of sheer gratefulness for how He accepts me so unconditionally. I've heard some people refer to this time in their lives as "open heart surgery". . . not a bad description. . .

> **Heb 10:22** Let us draw near with a true heart in full assurance of faith, having our hearts sprinkled from an evil conscience, and our bodies washed with pure water.
>
> **Jeremiah 30:18-22** Thus saith the LORD; Behold, I will bring again the captivity of Jacob's tents, and have mercy on his dwellingplaces; and the city shall be builded upon her own heap, and the palace shall remain after the manner

thereof. [19]And out of them shall proceed thanksgiving and the voice of them that make merry: and I will multiply them, and they shall not be few; I will also glorify them, and they shall not be small. [20]Their children also shall be as aforetime, and their congregation shall be established before me, and I will punish all that oppress them. [21]And their nobles shall be of themselves, and their governor shall proceed from the midst of them; and I will cause him to draw near, and he shall approach unto me: for who is this that engaged his heart to approach unto me? saith the LORD. [22]And ye shall be my people, and I will be your God.

I got a heart touch as God met us at choir one night. . . I felt it. . . He's so quick to meet me now. . . How many times has He said, draw near to me and I will draw near to you? It's as if I spent all my saved years never realizing, and somehow assuming that He didn't really mean what He said, or that it was some ethereal thing that didn't touch me right where the seat of my emotions are, right where my desires and longings are, touching my need for Him in a totally irresistible way.

As I've said before, the almost-tangible hugs God now gives me from time to time are such that a man would have to completely dislocate every muscle and bone in his body to even attempt something close to it! I wish those hugs would never end. . . I wish I could feel this closeness every waking moment. . .

To read Scriptures referenced in this chapter,
please visit http://songdove.fa-ct.com/
There you will find interactive Scripture references, videos containing lyrics to most of the songs in these chapters, topics mentioned in this chapter, and more.

Scriptures used, referred to or that relate to thoughts in this session:

Psalm 73:28   Isaiah 29:13
Mark 6:46   Hebrews 10:22
Jeremiah 30:21

Topics discussed, referred to, or that relate to thoughts in this session:

Fear/Shame   Gratitude
Unknown – change, fear   Pride versus humbleness – willingness
alabaster box   Obedience, humbleness, surrender
Submission/Trust   Brokenness
Trust – surrender   Remain open during trials and tests
Trust-peace-rest

Questions for Discussion:

What fears come to mind when you think of drawing near to God?

_____

_____

Is there anything that causes you to feel shame before God? _____

_____

How does God respond to your fear and shame?

_____

_____

Personal Acceptance:

> **Psalm 139:1-5** To the chief Musician, A Psalm of David. O
> LORD, thou hast searched me, and known me. ²Thou
> knowest my downsitting and mine uprising, thou under-
> standest my thought afar off. ³Thou compassest my path
> and my lying down, and art acquainted with all my ways.
> ⁴For there is not a word in my tongue, but, lo, O LORD,
> thou knowest it altogether. ⁵Thou hast beset me behind and
> before, and laid thine hand upon me.

The first 5 verses of Psalm 139 could be taken one of two ways depending
on the posture of a person's heart toward their Lord. The self-contained,
self-sustaining heart could take offence at these verses, feeling violated that
God knows so much about them and actively searches out their deepest,
darkest, hidden thoughts, feelings and intents, or motives. They could see
God as hemming them in and preventing them from exploring the freedom
they feel they'd otherwise have, bucking against the traces as it were. But then
there is the viewpoint that hit me over the head back in 2007, and that actually came as a comfort to me. A comfort that I found strange at first, but that
I quickly learned would become the new normal in my life as I sought to understand it. . .

God's knowledge of the deepest parts of me grants Him the ability to guide
and protect me in ways no human ever will. There is a vulnerability in that
discovery for sure. God has a way of dealing with anything in a person's life
that He finds will harm them. As the true parent God is, He will seek to
shield His children from sinful pursuits that stain their souls, and clean and
remove those stains already there. Sometimes a child will wait too long before showing a parent that they fell and scraped themselves, causing bits of
dirt to be mingled in with the scabbed blood. When the parent goes to clean
the scrape, they find they have to loosen the scab to get the dirt out or risk infection, but because the scab already dried, it can hurt.

The child has two choices, with the parent actively advocating the second choice for the good of the child. The child can either resist and push the parent away, trying to avoid the pain of the cleansing, or the child can comply no matter how much it might hurt and find comfort and healing in the process.

> **Psalm 139: 5** Thou has beset me behind and before, and laid Thine hand upon me

Verse 5 stood out to me back in May of '07 even more so than the knowledge that God knows the deepest parts of my thoughts and my heart. I found this verse to be especially comforting, considering I'd just come through what I've dubbed the second darkest storm of my entire life to this point. I needed God's comfort something fierce, which is one reason I think He showed up as He did. But to read how He surrounds me, hemming me in as it were and placing His hand upon me. . . that gave me a picture of a path, and my God not only covering me, but choosing to be my fore and rear guard. Other places in Scripture speak of my God being my buckler and my shield, my rear Guard, my strong tower, my fortress, my shelter, etc.

Needless to say verse 5 was added to my list of favourite verses from Scripture! There is safety under His wings, there is security found in His heart, all I have to be is open to Him, vulnerable to Him to receive those blessings. . . knowing full well that He may find things there that displease and cause Him to spring into action cleansing them from my life. . . but the healing and comfort are beyond words. . . the safety and security found in His arms I can't fully describe. . . I should know, I could fill a book with the words I've attempted in the past. . .

I find it timely that I come to this chapter at the beginning of 2011. Much has happened in the past year and I need the reassurance that God is still surrounding me, still has His hand on me, still has me under His wing. . . Such a quieting place to be. . .

To read Scriptures referenced in this chapter,
please visit http://songdove.fa-ct.com/
There you will find interactive Scripture references, videos containing lyrics to
most of the songs in these chapters, topics mentioned in this chapter, and
more.

Scriptures used, referred to or that relate to thoughts in this session:

Psalm 139

Topics discussed, referred to, or that relate to thoughts in this session:

Surrender	Gratitude
Forgiveness	Provision
Fear/Shame	Pride versus humbleness – willingness
Submission/Trust	Obedience, humbleness, surrender
Trust – surrender	Remain open during trials and tests
Trust-peace-rest	

Questions for Discussion:

Take some time to read all of Psalm 139. . . Which verse(s) stand out to you
the most (try not to be cliche)? Why?

_____

Do you find God's hand of protection and guidance limiting or comforting?
Explain. . .

_____

Has God ever had to clean dirt out of a wound in your life?

_____

Are there areas God longs to cleanse in your life?

_____

Even Darkness is Light to Thee

> **Psalm 139:6-12** Such knowledge is too wonderful for me; it is high, I cannot attain unto it. ⁷Whither shall I go from thy spirit? or whither shall I flee from thy presence? ⁸If I ascend up into heaven, thou art there: if I make my bed in hell, behold, thou art there. ⁹If I take the wings of the morning, and dwell in the uttermost parts of the sea; ¹⁰Even there shall thy hand lead me, and thy right hand shall hold me. ¹¹If I say, Surely the darkness shall cover me; even the night shall be light about me. ¹²Yea, the darkness hideth not from thee; but the night shineth as the day: the darkness and the light are both alike to thee.

Just thinking a little about the next few verses here. . . from verse 6 to 12. . . Verse 6 echoes Isaiah as the psalmist observes "Such knowledge is too wonderful for me; it is high, I cannot attain unto it." Isaiah tells us that God's ways are higher than our ways, and His thoughts higher than our thoughts. It is true that on our own, we cannot reach or understand how God thinks and does things, and yet He has revealed these to us in His Word. God has made Himself known to us through the pages of Scripture. Even then, it has taken many a lifetime to fully grasp just who God is and how He does things. God is just too big for anyone to feel they have a handle on the full breadth of all that goes on in the heart and mind of our Creator!

Then as if God's omniscient ways were not enough for the psalmist to mull over in one sitting, he takes off on another trail amazed at how God is everywhere, or omnipresent as we typically call it, in verses 7 - 12. It's worth thinking about, because too often, we think we can hide from God. As preposterous as that is in light of God's omnipresence, somehow mankind thinks that hiding from God is no different than hiding from another human or creature. Even Adam and Eve after they fell in the garden, thought they could hide from God.

But even in that story in the early chapters of Genesis, we see God's desire for relationship with His prize creation. It's not that God didn't know where Adam and Eve were hiding. He wanted them to admit their attempt and willingly come out into the open to commune with Him as they had done in times past. We must remember that there is no relationship if one person is doing all the talking, doing all the walking, and putting out all the effort. A relationship of any sort requires interaction on the part of two or more people. A loving relationship between parent and children for example, or between husband and wife. God says in various places of Scripture, "draw nigh to me and I will draw near to you." In other words, if we truly want relationship with God, if we want His presence in our lives, we need to show Him by putting a foot forward, by acting on that desire, proving that this is indeed what we really want. So He waited for Adam and Eve to come out of hiding, and He waits for us to come out of hiding as well.

> **Psalms 139:10-11** Even there shall thy hand lead me, and thy right hand shall hold me. ¹¹If I say, Surely the darkness shall cover me; even the night shall be light about me.

Jonah thought he could run away from God, Elijah ran into the desert hoping to die. . . why we think we can run away from God and hide is shown to be pure folly in light of the psalmist's words in these verses. There truly is something comforting about the fact that no matter where I am in this world, no matter how far away I think I am, God is there leading me and holding me. . . Such a thought draws me nearer. . . I want to be near the Lover of my soul, the Lord of my life, the King of my heart, and the Creator of the Universe. . . It still awes and amazes me that as God overseas the vastness of His creation, He chooses to come near, to draw me into His embrace, wanting intimate relationship with me! One day, my Bible tells me, He will put on the biggest marriage banquet the world has ever seen as He takes the Bride of Christ as wife and sits Her on His right hand forever more. Why would I want to hide from that? From the Author and Finisher of my faith?

It is when I fully grasp these verses and the futility of thinking I can hide anything from my Lord, that opening up the darkest recesses of my heart becomes easier to do, realizing that there really is no point to attempting the locking away of such things. Attempts to keep such things away from my Lord only leads to tears in His eyes, and pain in mine as I try to move forward with locks all over my heart. God longs to be King over my entire heart, not just the areas I think are safe to give Him.

In fact when God first brought this chapter to me in May of 2007, I didn't fully get His point, thinking before I even opened to the page in my Bible that I already knew this. Why did I need to go over it again? While I've read my Bible through a number of times over the years, for some reason the rest of this chapter had faded into my memory and all I could remember were the verses I'm about to go over in the next study. Even passages of Scripture can suffer stereotyping. . .

To read Scriptures referenced in this chapter,
please visit http://songdove.fa-ct.com/
There you will find interactive Scripture references, videos containing lyrics to most of the songs in these chapters, topics mentioned in this chapter, and more.

Scriptures used, referred to or that relate to thoughts in this session:

Isaiah 29:13   Psalm 139
Hebrews 10:22

Topics discussed, referred to, or that relate to thoughts in this session:

Fear/Shame	Gratitude
Unknown – change, fear	Pride versus humbleness – willingness
Submission/Trust	Obedience, humbleness, surrender
Trust – surrender	Letting God live through us
Trust-peace-rest	Remain open during trials and tests

Questions for Discussion:

Have you ever felt like hiding from God? _____

_____

Were you successful? _____

_____

What does God long for? _____

Using the online study search tool on the website or the nearest Strong's Concordance, locate the verses where Jonah tried to run from God, and where Elijah tried to run away. List them below:

_____

_____

How did God deal with Jonah? _____

_____

How did God deal with Elijah? _____

_____

God knows every single tiny detail of who I am, physically and spiritually.

> **Psalm 139:13-16** For thou hast possessed my reins: thou hast covered me in my mother's womb. [14]I will praise thee; for I am fearfully and wonderfully made: marvellous are thy works; and that my soul knoweth right well. [15]My substance was not hid from thee, when I was made in secret, and curiously wrought in the lowest parts of the earth. [16]Thine eyes did see my substance, yet being unperfect; and in thy book all my members were written, which in continuance were fashioned, when as yet there was none of them.

My focus the following morning was on verses 13 - 16. Typically when the term "reins" is used in reference to a person, it speaks of their will, their actions and their desires. When I hand someone my reins, I am referring to handing them a certain level of control over my actions, passions, and desires. I've met very few people who I felt qualified to be given such sway in my life, and those I have met have been very dear to me to say the least! But here I read that God possessed those reins, even while I was still in my mother's womb, God says He covered me. . . It's an interesting thought to consider that before each of us was born, God was in control of our lives, that even in the womb, God was there protecting and covering us. . .

Verse 16 tells us that not only is God in control, but that He wrote all our parts into a book before we were even formed! Kind of makes me think of a master craftsman making notes, sketches and blueprints before he sets to work actually building the final product. Our God is The Master Craftsman, carefully noting every intricate part of us before we are even knit together in our mother's womb!

When I read this again for the first time back in 2007, the bombshell to hit me over the head was that God delighted to form me how He did.

From age 12 onward, I hated the less-than-stellar attention I'd get from men because of my appearance. I couldn't walk downtown without getting whistled at, was stalked when I was 19, and a few years after I got married when I complained to my ex (husband at the time) that I should throw on burlap sacks and walk downtown that way, he didn't help matters by telling me that it doesn't matter what I wear, a man can still tell how I'm shaped! Now I'm no model, I'm no pin-up or anything, I hate having my picture taken for starters. . . but that kind of attention resulted in me secretly loathing the form I'd been given for many years.

As God was about to take me into spiritual boot camp, the first lesson I had to learn, was that God Himself delighted to give me this form! It pleased my Creator, my unseen Lover, to give me this shape, and that it was for His pleasure ultimately more than any pleasure any man would derive. I had to mull that one over for awhile. . . for almost 3 weeks at least before God would let me move on to the next challenge He would take me through. It was a bit of a harsh light bulb to realize that ALL of me, not just my heart, was created to please God, including my appearance, the way He formed me. That actually threw me for a bit of a tailspin for a few months, but it's true. If I truly believe that I was created for God's pleasure, that includes every single visible and invisible aspect of who I am!

> **1 Corinthians 6:19-20** What? know ye not that your body is the temple of the Holy Ghost which is in you, which ye have of God, and ye are not your own? [20]For ye are bought with a price: therefore glorify God in your body, and in your spirit, which are God's.

I finally stumbled on why it's so important that I accept the tent He made for me. . . It's HIS!!! He lives in it! In me! Refusing to accept the bodily tent He gave me is rejecting His handiwork, but more than that, rejecting it has lowered how I look after it, doing the basics but absolutely no more than that! If God is pleased to call this tent home, if He was pleased to make it in this shape, then He's the only opinion that matters! I can quit being so upset over how others have treated me in their imaginations and actions and instead focus on God's opinion of me, because this body is His! I can be such a slow learner sometimes! I have a lot of relearning to do now because there is no reason to hide myself from God. There is no longer any reason for me to hide behind refusal to adorn myself. . .

We take great care to look after the houses we build for God out of wood and steel, and King Solomon's Temple was the most beautiful building of its time. Taking minimal care of this biological temple rather than taking the same level of care for it as I do for the building down the street is kind of pulling the same manoeuvre that upsets me in my son. Doing the bare minimum doesn't say much about my stewardship if it's done in my finances or any other resource in my possession.

For years I have forgotten this is His habitation, His home, His Temple, and have thought all this time I was trying to hide from opinions and attention from a sector of society that has no say in what God has or has not given me!!! Oh I could hug someone for this revelation!!!

If I truly believe **Psalm 139:16**, then that affects how I look after what God has given me. I'm not just looking after my body because that's the healthy thing to do. I'm not adorning and clothing it just because it's the morally right thing to do. My body becomes a house as Scripture sometimes calls it, that is given to me to steward, to manage, to look after, for the Master, for the Head of the Home. I'm not managing it for the attention of men, although many women have an unhealthy attachment between how men view their appearance and their self-worth. I'm managing it for the One who gave it to me, for the One who took pleasure in plotting out my frame on his blueprint and forming me according to the plans and notes written in His Book! Scripture tells me that if I look for the praise of men, that I have my reward, but if I look for the praise of God, that the rewards in heaven will vastly outweigh anything here on earth!

Does God care about my physical appearance? If we think of caring about my appearance based on the world's definition, the answer would be no. God told Samuel that while man looks on the outward appearance, God looks on the heart. God told Solomon that favour is fleeting and beauty is vain, but the woman who fears the Lord will be praised. God had Paul write to a church urging women to put less emphasis on decorating their hair and more emphasis on presenting a heart pleasing to God. At first glance then, one could get the impression that if God puts so much more emphasis on the state of our hearts, that we can do whatever we please with the tent God built for us and God won't care.

But God does care! How we treat our bodies is an indication of what goes on in our hearts. How we treat the bodies of others is also an indication of what is going on in our hearts. God tells the husband and wife that their bodies are not for themselves but for each other and not to deprive one another. God went to great lengths in the Law to teach the Hebrew people how to look after themselves hygienically, how to handle infection, germs, menstruation, illness, where to put the washrooms, how to prepare food, etc. Many of those laws have shaped the levels of hygiene we now see in today's homes and hospitals around the world. They are not laws unto salvation, they are what I'd call hygienic laws.

God cares that women dress modestly and that men and women do not wear each other's clothing. Some groups of Christians take this to extremes and do not consider what is men's and women's clothing in the cultures to which they belong or to which they travel. In Western society, we have jeans for men and women, but they are cut drastically different! In some of the middle eastern countries, there are robes for both men and women, but they are cut and shaped quite differently. Men are to wear the clothes built for men, and women are to wear the clothes built for women. It doesn't matter what culture you're from, each culture knows what men and women are to wear in that culture.

God even cares about adornment. I've read various places in Scripture where God speaks to Israel and Jerusalem, and a few times even the Church, in the manner of a King adorning His Bride. It keeps slipping my mind, but one day I want to go back through those passages and study what each type of raiment and adornment stands for in the life of the Christian. God isn't against adornment. His Bride will be the most beautifully adorned being the world has ever seen! All of today's glitz and glamour will pale in comparison when She comes to the Marriage Supper of the Lamb! God is merely against adornment for the praise of men, saying such is fleeting and vain.

It boils down to who we are pleasing when we get up in the morning. It boils down to who the focus is in our heart and mind. If I wake up wanting to please my Lord, I will look after myself accordingly. If I wake up wanting to please the men downtown (God forbid), I will clothe and adorn myself accordingly. If I wake up and could care less who I please (and I've been there), my appearance will reflect that.

So knowing all this, knowing that God controlled, planned, wrote down, and built me from the ground up to be who I am and look how I do, who does my appearance reflect? Whose praise am I seeking to earn? Whose pleasure am I desirous to enter into? The answer will decide how I look after myself!

A Prayer:
Oh Lord, I think I finally understand, I think I finally got it! My body is Yours. My heart, soul, mind and spirit are all Yours! Oh God, I need not fear what man may think of me, I have only to desire what You think of me, and that includes my outward appearance, the tent You built for me! Oh God, help me to work this out, to be pleasing to You in how I adorn this Temple. It had nothing to do with sexuality! It had everything to do with Your habitation within me!!! Oh God, forgive me for being so blind, forgive me for being so questioning, oh God, thank You for Your patience, and for the patience of my pastor as the poor guy gets subjected to such crazy things from this head and heart of mine!
***

To read Scriptures referenced in this chapter,
please visit http://songdove.fa-ct.com/
There you will find interactive Scripture references, videos containing lyrics to
most of the songs in these chapters, topics mentioned in this chapter, and
more.

Scriptures used, referred to or that relate to thoughts in this session:

Psalm 139   1 Timothy 2:9
1 Corinthians 3:16   1 Peter 3:3
1 Corinthians 9:13   1 Corinthians 7:2-16
1 Samuel 16:7   Romans 12:1
Proverbs 31:30

Topics discussed, referred to, or that relate to thoughts in this session:

Offering self as an act of worship   Stewardship of the body
Self-acceptance – Surrender   Pride versus humbleness – willingness
Fear/Shame   Obedience, humbleness, surrender

Questions for Discussion:

What does Romans 12:1 mean to you? _____

_____

What does it mean when Scripture asks if we understand that we are the
Temple of the Holy Ghost? How do we show that understanding?

_____

Where should our focus be when we consider how to look after these bodies
God has given us?

_____

_____

Take a moment to examine how you currently look after yourself. Would you say your stewardship of your body honours God or man?

What are some ways you can ensure that stewardship of your body honours God above all others?

Epilogue for this study session:

Well, a year later, and much to my amazement, my manner of dress has been changing, not a lot, but noticeable enough for me. Change number one has been how I dress in the summertime. I used to be a t-shirt and shorts girl. But beginning with summer 2007 with one article of clothing, that moved to two articles in summers, 2008 and 2009 I have found myself more comfortable in sleeveless sun-dresses! I have to admit that my appearance in these things is softer and more pleasing to the eye than the t-shirts and shorts I used to wear all the time. Change number two happened in 2008, as I wore a satchel with broken zippers for 6 months, left it at home while going to Rwanda, and came back from Rwanda with a travel purse! It's a camping-green coloured thing, not flashy, "pretty" or attractive, but its functional, and has to be worn across the shoulder and chest. This meant no more satchel tied to my waist until I found another one with a stronger zipper in 2011.

But back in those earlier years, the thought going through my head when I realized what was happening was, "oh my goodness!!! I'm feminizing!!!" . . . Now that may make some people laugh who have known me for a long time. . . but this is a big deal! I haven't abandoned my jeans or sweatshirts or turtlenecks.

In fact God brought more of those my way weeks before I left for Rwanda! So He must like me in those clothes too. But the point here, for me at least, is that when I released my appearance into God's hands, sure enough. . . in no rush but definitely taking action. . . God began to change my wardrobe, began to change how I see myself!

Speaking of seeing myself, I had another startling wake-up moment after I got back from Rwanda in 2008. I was looking through the pictures of me handing out certificates and receiving my farewell gift, when I caught myself actually enjoying those pictures!!! For the first time that I can remember, my gut reaction was, "I look good in that picture!, I like that picture of me!!! I could hardly believe my thoughts!!! I literally did a double-take! For the first time in my life. . . I like how I looked in these pictures!!! This too is a huge thing for me and only those who know of my hatred and dislike for cameras will understand how huge this is!

I can't help thinking if part or all of those thoughts were actually God telling me what He thinks of me in those pictures. Telling me I'm beautiful. I had a dream one summer where I'd asked God as I wore the first of the two sundresses, "Daddy, do you think I'm pretty?" I cried in that dream, I could barely get those words out of my mouth and I woke up in tears. Now it seems I am hearing God's answer. I was taken by surprise, but along with that surprise has come a comforting feeling to my heart. . . a feeling that I am pleasing to my Lord in the way He made me and in how He is covering me and adorning me. Indeed you can't get much better than having God as your clothier and tailor. I had always fought with the fact that men found me attractive, refusing to accept it for myself, looking in the mirror half the time, wondering what they saw. But it's hard to buck when God is the one whispering in your ear, when God is the one changing your heart and perspective.
***

Freedom in Surrendering my Body:

My body is God's, not mine. It's not men's opinions I have to be concerned about, it's God's opinion. You have no idea how this feels unless you've faced this issue yourself at some point in your past. If I'd come to this conclusion in person, you'd see me beaming! This is what God wanted!!! Give Him the burden of my scars and wounds. I think I finally did that. . . Once again I feel both happy and quieted all at the same time! Guess female emotions have something contradictory all the time eh? Happy and quiet all at the same time. . .

Submitting my body to God has had a marked change in my thought/dream life. I never associated having to hand over my body and all that's built into its functionality, with asking God to take control of my longings and desires of this heart. Everyone always talks about taking every thought captive to the Holy Spirit, but I have never heard anyone teach that some thoughts and desires are directly related to our bodies' natural desires, the hormonal desires. To bring those desires captive, we have to lay our bodies at the foot of the Cross, not just our mind and heart. But this is what had to happen for me.

I had to submit my body to Christ.

> **Romans 12:1** I beseech you therefore, brethren, by the mercies of God, that ye present your bodies a living sacrifice, holy, acceptable unto God, which is your reasonable service.

Seeking to please God in my body with its desires and longings is desiring to be holy in this aspect of life. I knew what I wanted before God, and God knew what I wanted, but I was misunderstanding how He said to address it, repeatedly. I was completely missing the point of what He wanted from me. Now that I finally understand, I can present my body to Him with the desire of living holy before Him in my heart and thoughts and desires. I wonder if that's why the cleansing seemed to happen so quickly, and so noticeably!

I can't say I've ever felt a sudden cleanness come over me like that before! This must be what some people who have spent half their lives in sin have felt when they've described coming to Christ and feeling as if they've just been washed from head to toe. I used to think that was admirable talk and quaint, having never felt it for myself. I mean, at the age of 7, how much sin does the average kid get themselves into? But I freshly presented my body to God one night, and there was a major difference in how I found my personal desires behaving. This is one of those areas requiring repeated submission I am discovering, as months turn into years after this initial discovery. But God is there, willing to answer when I finally lower my head and heart before Him and submit to His cleansing fire.

Reinforcing the Lesson

I know I have some working out to do in living with a healthier view of this human tent. But I'm not going to rush it. After having given this body to God, He may have ideas of His own for how I should move forward in working out how I live in this new reality. And new reality it is for me. I'm not joking when the thoughts that plagued me began when I was 12. The fact those thoughts were fed repeatedly as I grew up and later by how my ex treated me, is very real. But God wanted to heal that, and as with anything He wants to heal, He can't heal it till we give it to Him! I keep telling people that if they want God to heal something, to give it to Him. It really does help to follow my own advice!!! I found myself looking for those scars and wounds again. . . I see shadows of where they were? My mentor saw me fight with these rather harshly when a guy was trying to win me! He (my mentor) heard me talk about these hurts when I shared my story with him. I've lived with them for a long time! But. . . this lightness, this quietness. . . that's the word. . . not shutdown. . . quieted. . . my desires have been quieted. I shake my head in amazement. . . God is moving so fast in my life right now! I may be slow on the uptake, but He's most assuredly not!

To read Scriptures referenced in this chapter,
please visit http://songdove.fa-ct.com/
There you will find interactive Scripture references, videos containing lyrics to
most of the songs in these chapters, topics mentioned in this chapter, and
more.

Scriptures used, referred to or that relate to thoughts in this session:

Romans 12:1   Galatians 5:24
John :13   Romans 8:13
Galatians 5:13

Topics discussed, referred to, or that relate to thoughts in this session:

Offering self as an act of worship   Trust – surrender
Self-acceptance – Surrender   Pride versus humbleness – willingness
Stewardship of the body   Obedience, humbleness, surrender
Submission/Trust

Questions for Discussion:

What does Romans 12:1 mean to you? _____

_____

Scripture refers to flesh as: flesh of animals, flesh as in one's kin, flesh as in
carnal or sinful desires and "flesh and blood" as in one's own body. Verses
given could be saying that what society calls "instinct", might be sin's effects
on our natural desires. What do you think?

_____

_____

Scripture says if we walk after the Spirit we won't be afflicted with the desires of the flesh. How is this so?

_____

_____

Where there's a Shadow, there's a Light:

They say shadows don't fall unless there is a light behind the object casting the shadow. I know the source of that light, and that source is One who has chosen to be called after the male gender. He has shown me a taste of His intimate love for me and wants to take me deeper. His call to prepare for going deeper sent me into an evening of misunderstandings one night, hurt questions, and puzzled feelings and thoughts. But getting past that appeared to begin the healing process where suddenly I didn't see the scars but saw shadows of where they were. Now to get past those shadows, now to get past the memories and hurts that show up at times. Oh God help me. . .

I have been bowing my head toward the Lord, renewing my submission to His will without knowing the answers. *sigh* Trust without answers. . . to put feet to trusting that God knows what He's doing even when I can't see it for myself. I'm in need of His comfort in a big way. I've pretty much been in a raw state beginning with the regret issue (motherhood in case the reader has lost track).

Perhaps all these new experiences will pull me out faster than in times past. "Voice of Truth" just came on. . . *sigh* Oh God help me get through this. . .

> **Ephesians 5:2** And walk in love, as Christ also hath loved us, and hath given himself for us an offering and a sacrifice to God for a sweetsmelling savour.

> **Philippians 4:18** But I have all, and abound: I am full, having received of Epaphroditus the things which were sent from you, an odour of a sweet smell, a sacrifice acceptable, wellpleasing to God.

One Mother's Day the concept of giving myself as a rose to Christ hit me over the head. . . It was a concept I hadn't considered, and yet we sing about our praise being a sweet smelling fragrance before the Lord. We read in Scripture about presenting our bodies being a pleasing act before the Lord.

> **Romans 12:1** I beseech you therefore, brethren, by the mercies of God, that ye present your bodies a living sacrifice, holy, acceptable unto God, *which is* your reasonable service.

The concept that presenting ourselves, our entire self, body, soul and spirit as an act that brings personal pleasure to God is something that up to now has been mostly head knowledge and not something that I really took as being so intimately personal either on my end or God's. The thought that His prize creation willingly, of its own choosing, offers itself totally and completely to Him in every way possible producing a sense of personal pleasure in God Himself is yet another new thought for this heart to comprehend.

God's Emotions:

It almost humanizes God that He'd respond to such an act of devotion. Perhaps that's because I'm still getting used to the fact that God's emotions are not just ethereal, but very real, very touchable. . . and very intense. . . Somehow I keep forgetting that God made us "in His image", meaning He had emotions before we did and models the sinless way of using them!!! There is something in the human heart that is set off in a manner of reciprocated unexplainable devotion and commitment when one person gives themselves wholly over to the other person for their pleasure. The person receiving such devotion wants to return it, wants to protect it, wants to care for it, wants to cherish it. Why on earth would I think God would respond any less??? If anything, I should be anticipating that He'd not only respond in this manner, but even more so! The limits of the human mind and heart can be frustrating at times! The Creator of our feelings and emotions, feels them just as much as we do, but without sin, and with more passion and intensity!

If only it were possible to feel things the way God does, I might not be so scared to feel half the time nor would I go overboard when I do let myself feel.

Indeed my life is not my own. The more I enter into this new space in His love, the more I'm realizing it will never be my own. I just do whatever He brings me to do, say whatever He gives me to say, and that's it. This does feel like another sacrifice. . . Some doors shut and never reopen. Some comfort zones don't let you back in after you leave them. I need to engage in another bout of surrender here. There is sadness as I consider it, but I can't hold onto what won't open up to me. What matters is that I quit wishing I could resurrect what I once had, and do my best to accept and enjoy what God's given me now.

Lord of the Dance:

One morning I daydreamed about doing something I've never done before! I saw myself with a guy who had his hands on my hips and was guiding me in a slow dance-style sway. The look on his face was one of gentle, loving command. He was in control of the dance and was asking me to follow along, to give in to the movements he dictated. Now I've never danced in my life (unless gym class in elementary school counts), so dreaming about it was very different. I found myself staring into his eyes and starting to lose myself in the love I saw there when the daydream was interrupted with activity around me.

The thought came to me that this is what Christ wants from me. He wants to be in control, to be the One in command. He looks at me with loving gentleness and asks that I yield to His hands as He guides my movements. As Steven Curtis Chapman sang, Jesus is Lord of the Dance. I ask God for help in learning to yield to His control of my life.

One day I was rereading a chapter in the book, "Journey of the Bride", telling God I don't want to be as the Shulamite maiden in those verses, hiding behind her wall and telling the King to go on without her. I want to go when I'm called and be obedient to what He asks of me. While the unknown can be a source of adventure, it is also a source of uncertainty and fear. I've never shied from change before, typically looking at it as adventure. But maybe due to life experiences. . . change now brings with it more stresses than I remember. It's timely that God would be teaching me about trust, peace, rest, and His love.

I don't know what He has planned for me, but change continues to be in the wind. I still can't fathom how prophetic that 2006 Christmas-break comment would be, that 2007 would be a year of social and emotional upheaval. I had no idea what I was talking about or what would come down the pipe. This call to step out has been confirmed in so many ways lately, from songs to Scripture passages to the writings of others, including my own fingers.

When the Lord of the Dance says to move to a certain way in a certain direction, it is time to follow His hand, all the while keeping my eyes fixed on that gentle commanding gaze. . . My God knows best.

To view lyrics for songs referenced in this chapter,
please visit http://songdove.fa-ct.com/
There you will find interactive Scripture references, videos containing lyrics to most of the songs listed here, topics mentioned in this chapter, and more.

Scriptures used, referred to or that relate to thoughts in this session:

Romans 12:1   Philippians 4:18
Ephesians 5:2

Songs shared, referenced, or that relate to thoughts in this session:

Voice of Truth   Lord of the Dance

Topics discussed, referred to, or that relate to thoughts in this session:

Offering self as an act of worship   Trust-peace-rest
Unknown – change, fear   Pride versus humbleness – willingness
Stewardship of the body   Obedience, humbleness, surrender
Submission/Trust   Letting God live through us
Trust – surrender   Remain open during trials and tests

Questions for Discussion:

Have you ever thought of pleasing God with your body? Yes _____ No _____

What does it mean to present ourselves as living sacrifices?

_____

_____

What are some of the emotions God displays in Scripture? Use the study search tool on the website or the nearest Strong's Concordance to give examples.

_____

_____

_____

_____

Gratitude for God's Provision:

For all of my failings, for all of my humanity, for all of my struggles, the fact God sees fit to provide for the kids and I as He does is indeed cause for much gratitude, thanksgiving and appreciation. I don't deserve half of what God's brought my way, don't deserve the extras He's allowed into our lives. . . Who would have thought the kids would be given such incredible opportunities?! In an age of shifting employment landscapes, I had the same contractual boss for 6 years. God answering my prayer for favour with the landlord and neighbours in the building is something that in my own flesh is totally unmerited. But the fact God has seen fit even to offer these extras causes fresh bouts of thanksgiving to come forward whenever I stop to think about it and I think about it at least 3 times a day.

The day I lose sight of God's provision in our lives is the day I fall with pride, self-sufficiency, and the day my independent spirit wins out over this increasing desire to submit and humble myself before God and His purposes. I know my independence and self-sufficient attempts have been things God has not been overly pleased with. On the one hand they've combined with my strong-willed driven nature to allow me to forge ahead when others would have landed in the psych ward at the hospital. They combined to keep me moving when I would have otherwise curled up on my bed and never roused again. They combined to build determination that we would not live on welfare forever, but would get off it as soon as possible, bucking the defeating methods they employ and getting off it within a year of going on.

Struggle #2: Finances:

Yet at the same time I can't attribute everything in those times to myself. It was also during those times where God forcefully taught me that I had to look to Him for our provision and the longer I refused, the deeper we fell into financial trouble till finally in November of 2002, there was absolutely no way rent would be paid, groceries bought or bills paid. I finally admitted I couldn't provide for the kids myself.

I finally admitted that only God could keep us going. Then three different groups of people came along, none of them knowing each other or even being aware of each other, and rent, bills and groceries were provided for us! God did something similar to make sure we got through December of that year. Then the week of boxing day(the day after Christmas on some calendars), God brought three contracts along! One of those contracts remains with me to this day, and one of them had something for me to do almost every day of the week until cancer took them in September of 2010.

> **Matthew 6:25-34** Therefore I say unto you, Take no thought for your life, what ye shall eat, or what ye shall drink; nor yet for your body, what ye shall put on. Is not the life more than meat, and the body than raiment? [26]Behold the fowls of the air: for they sow not, neither do they reap, nor gather into barns; yet your heavenly Father feedeth them. Are ye not much better than they? [27]Which of you by taking thought can add one cubit unto his stature? [28]And why take ye thought for raiment? Consider the lilies of the field, how they grow; they toil not, neither do they spin: [29]And yet I say unto you, That even Solomon in all his glory was not arrayed like one of these. [30]Wherefore, if God so clothe the grass of the field, which to day is, and to morrow is cast into the oven, shall he not much more clothe you, O ye of little faith? [31]Therefore take no thought, saying, What shall we eat? or, What shall we drink? or, Wherewithal shall we be clothed? [32](For after all these things do the Gentiles seek:) for your heavenly Father knoweth that ye have need of all these things. [33]But seek ye first the kingdom of God, and his righteousness; and all these things shall be added unto you. [34]Take therefore no thought for the morrow: for the morrow shall take thought for the things of itself. Sufficient unto the day is the evil thereof.

God had to teach me financial reliance on Him. That was a very big lesson for me! The concept of asking others for help was also a lesson God was try-ing to get me to learn during those days. It's still something I often forget to do because I was raised to be self-sustaining.

These lessons combined with God periodically smashing my pride and for-cing me to humble myself toward others or toward Him have resulted in me finally reaching a point, a point that was sped up as a result of experiencing a greater measure of God's love in the spring of 2007, where I discovered that I want to humble myself before Him and others. Unfortunately "others" isn't as wide-reaching as it could be, or it would extend to those that get in my way and inconvenience me. But the desire is there in a greater measure toward my God-given authority figures at the very least. That is a start in itself, as part of my independent streak in times past would often lead to bucking authority if I felt I had a better handle on something than they did, or that I had a bet-ter way of doing something, etc.

To read Scriptures referenced in this chapter,
please visit http://songdove.fa-ct.com/
There you will find interactive Scripture references, videos containing lyrics to most of the songs in these chapters, topics mentioned in this chapter, and more.

Scriptures used, referred to or that relate to thoughts in this session:

Matthew 6:25-33

Topics discussed, referred to, or that relate to thoughts in this session:

Offering self as an act of worship	Provision
Surrender	Pride versus humbleness – willingness
Forgiveness	Obedience, humbleness, surrender
Gratitude	

Questions for Discussion:

What is your typical reaction when bills begin to pile up?

A) Gotta work more hours

B) Gotta cut back on something

C) Stress and or worry

D) Pray

E) Some combination of the above. . .

Reacting in that manner gives you comfort because:

A) It's how I always handle it

B) It gives me something tangible to deal with

C) God helps those who help themselves

D) Comfort??? Are you serious???

What does the passage in Matthew say our response should be?

_____

_____

What does your response to the above questions say about your level of trust in God's ability to meet your needs?

_____

_____

How has God met your needs in the past?

_____

Humility:

It truly is humbling to think that with all these wayward human behaviours, God has been so faithful, caring, protective and loving. . . This is why it blows me away so much that He introduced Himself as my unseen Husband!!! While I sometimes find myself longing for a second chance with an earthly mate, other times I look at myself and wonder why anyone would want to be with me. Looking at my humanity just makes it more amazing that Jesus wants me as His Bride. I don't know if I'll ever get over that amazement. He loves me in spite of everything I've felt, thought, said and done!

I feel guilty any time I take pride in what I do now. I've caught myself feeling like I should have kept my mouth shut a couple times over the past while when I talked about things I enjoy doing. I guess you could say I've swung the other way, gone from pride in what I've accomplished here and there, to being scared of showing any pride at all. There must be a healthy middle ground there someplace, because if we don't take a certain amount of healthy pride in what we do and how we do it, then we won't give our best effort or even be aware of what our best is. I know what my best is and I strive for it in ministry, on the job, etc., but I feel guilty describing it to others, as if I'm blowing my own horn. Even hearing others blow that horn for me gets embarrassing at times.

I just want to be allowed to do my best quietly, with little fanfare, that way I know I've hopefully managed to please God with my efforts without being embarrassed by public displays of thanks or gratitude.

Another daymare (nightmare during the day) hit me one time about being publicly thanked for something I'd done. Again in this dream I tried to run and hide. I was found of course, but I nearly shed real tears as I tried to explain to the one who found me why I didn't want to be hauled on the platform for what they wanted to say in public.

One time my senior pastor talked about people who carry out their tasks and never get publicly thanked for it. He was speaking to those who feel because they don't get thanked publicly that their efforts aren't recognized or appreciated. However I sat there and felt that I was enjoying the lack of public recognition because to me that is the better way to serve.

If I compare life now to life before the black blot, there is a resurrection of desires, only this time combined with a brokenness in my independence and self-sufficiency that wasn't there in years past. Maybe that's why it feels new. I grew up, graduated school, and led my life prior to my divorce in a very independent spirit. That spirit went with me into ministry, which led to a few situations here and there that I'm not proud of. So it is safe to say all this is a new experience, another level.

Willingness and Acceptance:

> **Philippians 2:12-15** Wherefore, my beloved, as ye have always obeyed, not as in my presence only, but now much more in my absence, work out your own salvation with fear and trembling. [13]For it is God which worketh in you both to will and to do of his good pleasure. [14]Do all things without murmurings and disputings: [15]That ye may be blameless and harmless, the sons of God, without rebuke, in the midst of a crooked and perverse nation, among whom ye shine as lights in the world;

I'm still feeling like I've only just gotten past the acceptance and willingness phase. But wow! It really is as if that's all God wants from me! That all He wants is my willingness and acceptance of what He wants to do in my life!

I wonder if that's why so many things never get done by so many people, because we figure we are doing it on our own. . . as if God's told us to do something then stood back to see if we'll actually do it or not. In reality He longs to hold us through it, to love us through it, to give us the needed encouragement to accomplish it, but our spiritual eyes and ears are closed to this desired display in our lives, and we feel alone. Because we feel alone, the desired behaviour never gets acted on. We tell God we can't do it for a wide variety of reasons and all of them are perfectly justified from a human perspective.

Surrendering myself to this new experience in God's love has been producing changes in me that even my Grandma, who I don't talk to very often, can see at a simple glance. I'm sensing convictions so much more readily than I ever used to, God is revealing things to me, and finally brought me to the choice to forgive those I've had a really hard time forgiving. My Senior Pastor talked about loving the unlovable, loving our enemies, and in all honesty my ex had become my enemy and I've seen myself as unlovable, and at various times my Dad has seemed like an enemy. In order to love our enemies, we need to forgive them, even if that love is simply the Agape (see glossary on website if you'd like to learn about this kind of love) type and in no way related to any other form of love. . . to see and treat others and ourselves as God sees and treats us.

Struggle #3: Interpersonal Relations:

> **James 1:22** But be ye doers of the word, and not hearers only, deceiving your own selves.

I paused half way through answering questions in the guide for "Journey of the Bride" one morning, asking Christ to show me how to speak, to borrow my mouth for awhile and just let me watch, listen and observe how He does things as I let him speak through me. I learn by observation as much as I do by bookwork. Maybe watching Him interact through me will allow me to see where I've made mistakes in the past and how Christ handles it so I can improve in the future. If the gift of teaching is going to be revived, I can't deny that interpersonal skills are going to be necessary. I have no idea how that teaching will resurrect itself, will it remain one on one, will it move into group settings, I have no idea and I know that is one answer I should not strive to get. God will lead me into whatever situation He needs me in.

All I know is that I should not sit around and go "nice sermon God, well-written, good solid points, great punchline, I'll go eat lunch now". I need to act on this. Action involves service to others, it involves humble attitudes and behaviour, it involves obedience. . . I freely admit that without God taking control, I will fail again! So this also involves repeated surrender. If I once again try to move in interpersonal situations under my own control, I will mess up as I have at various times in my life so far, straining relationships of various types and descriptions, sometimes cutting those relationships off altogether because I could not handle situations with the needed grace and mercy called for.

How does a loner accomplish these goals, learn these lessons successfully, and adequately move about in a sea of faces? I know surrendering control to God and adopting a servant's heart are part of this. Is there more I need to be considering in the practical outworking of this God-delivered sermon?

To read Scriptures referenced in this chapter,
please visit http://songdove.fa-ct.com/
There you will find interactive Scripture references, videos containing lyrics to most of the songs in these chapters, topics mentioned in this chapter, and more.

Scriptures used, referred to or that relate to thoughts in this session:

Philippians 2:12-15   James 1:22

Topics discussed, referred to, or that relate to thoughts in this session:

Trust-peace-rest	Broken – independent spirit
Gratitude	Brokenness
Provision	Letting God live through us
Pride versus humbleness – willingness	Remain open during trials and tests
Obedience, humbleness, surrender	

Questions for Discussion:

Has God ever touched pride in your life? _____

_____

What are the differences between pride and humility? _____

_____

Using the search tool on the website or the nearest Strong's Concordance, what are some verses where God teaches us about human interaction?

_____

_____

Surrendering and Restoring My Dreams:

> **Psalm 84:10** For a day in thy courts is better than a thousand. I had rather be a doorkeeper in the house of my God, than to dwell in the tents of wickedness.

Another song has been speaking to me and echoing desires in my heart lately. "Give it all Away" by Aaron Shust: It sums up a lot of how I've been feeling toward the Lord, dreams that are resurrecting, plans, desires for cleansing and holiness before Him, etc.

For years I'd tell people that I don't really have any dreams, plans or goals anymore because of just trying to get from one day to the next providing for my children and seeking to be found in God's House. It didn't occur to me for awhile that seeking to be found in God's House was still a dream and a goal. Because I've grown up in Church, this was more of an enjoyable accepted/desired way of life than a dream or goal. But I've discovered that it is a dream that I began to find myself longing to realize again. If I could, I'd once again choose to "live" at the Church. I very quickly realized that I'd better let God control this dream. I spent time offering God these dreams, goals and plans, asking Him to take them and do with them as He will. I don't want to overstep Him, don't want to charge ahead without His leading anymore. Thus songs like the one above from Aaron Shust have taken on fresh meaning for me as I listen to them, adding them to my prayer of surrender.

I am brought to tears every time I consider or hear others talking about laying our dreams at the "Foot of the Cross", placing them in God's Hands, or before they get that far, watching dreams apparently die only to be revived and restored years later in ways they never dreamed of.

My tears come because I have lived this, and in some ways, still feel like I'm living it, so the tears are fresh every time. One dream that has not been restored to me is that of being happily married and immersed in ministry. That dream died when I realized the man I married would not appreciate my desire to be in God's House as often as I longed to be there. When I found myself divorced, that dream along with others involving ministry all died within me. It was a tearful death, but one I didn't see any way out of.

> **Joel 2:25** And I will restore to you the years that the locust hath eaten, the cankerworm, and the caterpiller, and the palmerworm, my great army which I sent among you.

God began to restore my use in ministry little by little, until just in the last few years, God sped things up and before I knew it I was subbing on the praise teams, working on the church website, helping with team communications, and eventually landing a part-time contract with the church office in the role of technical assistant. God didn't stop there, but began restoring ministries I hadn't engaged in since I was a child! I found myself subbing behind the sound booth computer, running the program responsible for all the songs, announcements and video displays. I found myself managing volume controls on the soundboard for a series of meetings and then in the sanctuary for a morning service. Then the most dramatic yet, God sent me on a short-term missions trip to Rwanda, effectively bringing full-circle my time growing up with my parents in various forms of home missions work! The skin colour was a bit darker, and the language different. The food was a little different but not by much. Conditions I encountered weren't unlike those I was used to among BC's coastal reserve communities.

And yet, with all that's been restored to me, tears still flow every time I hear people talk of seeing a dream, watching it die, or never realizing it in the first place and having to wait for what seems like forever before its finally realized in a manner the person never ever anticipated. This point was driven home all over again by the story shared about "The Three Trees" Tears wanted to flow then as well. I wish to share it here for my reader's review. . .

"The Three Trees" Author Unknown

Once there were three trees on a hill in a woods. They were discussing their hopes and dreams when the first tree said "Someday I hope to be a treasure chest. I could be filled with gold, silver and precious gems. I could be decorated with intricate carving and everyone would see the beauty." Then the second tree said "Someday I will be a mighty ship. I will take kings and queens across the waters and sail to the corners of the world. Everyone will feel safe in me because of the strength of my hull."

Finally the third tree said. "I want to grow to be the tallest and straightest tree in the forest. People will see me on top of the hill and look up to my branches, and think of the heavens and God and how close to them I am reaching. I will be the greatest tree of all time and people will always remember me."

After a few years of praying that their dreams would come true, a group of woodsmen came upon the trees. When one came to the first tree he said, "This looks like a strong tree, I think I should be able to sell the wood to a carpenter. and he began cutting it down. The tree was happy, because he knew that the carpenter would make him into a treasure chest.

At the second tree a woodsman said, "This looks like a strong tree, I should be able to sell it to the shipyard." The second tree was happy because he knew he was on his way to becoming a mighty ship. When the woodsmen came upon the third tree, the tree was frightened because he knew that if they cut him down his dreams would not come true. One of the woodsman said, "I don't need anything special from my tree so I'll take this one and he cut it down."

When the first tree arrived at the carpenters, he was made into a feed box for animals. He was then placed in a barn and filled with hay. This was not at all what he had prayed for.

The second tree was cut and made into a small fishing boat. His dreams of being a mighty ship and carrying kings had come to an end. The third tree was cut into large pieces and left alone in the dark.

The years went by, and the trees forgot about their dreams. Then one day, a man and women came to the barn. She gave birth and they placed the baby in the hay in the feed box that was made from the first tree. The man wished that he could have made a crib for the baby, but this manger would have to do. The tree could feel the importance of this event and knew that it had held the greatest treasure of all time.

Years later, a group of men got in the fishing boat made from the second tree. One of them was tired and went to sleep. While they were out on the water, a great storm arose and the tree didn't think it was strong enough to keep the men safe. The men woke the sleeping man, and he stood and said "peace" and the storm stopped.

At this time, the tree knew that it had carried the king of kings in its boat.

Finally, someone came and got the third tree. It was carried through the streets as the people mocked the man who was carrying it. When they came to a stop, the man was nailed to the tree and raised in the air to die at the top of a hill. When Sunday came, the tree came to realize that it was strong enough to stand at the top of the hill and be as close to God as was possible, because Jesus had been crucified on it."

The moral of this story is that when things don't seem to be going your way, always know that God has a plan for you. If you place your trust in Him, He will give you great gifts. Each of the trees got what they wanted, just not in the way they had imagined.

* * *

Will I realize my dream of being happily married in ministry? Is this a dream God will grant? I don't know. Right now that seems like an impossibility the way I understand my current marital condition according to Scripture. But God has made ways where there has seemed to be no way for people in times past. So who knows. . .

I am grateful for what God has restored in my life so far. It fills me with excitement and anticipation wondering what God will do next. . . where He'll take me next. . . what He'll get me doing next. . . But one thing's for sure, God isn't done with me yet. That thought helps to quiet the tears. He has my future.

Just as the three trees all realized their dreams in ways they never dreamed or anticipated, I can't help wondering how God will do things in my life in the future. I heard a phrase one time, a cliche that I don't hear anymore. "Expect the unexpected". . . God loves doing things in completely unorthodox ways! So to add another phrase, "Where are we going today?"

I don't know what God has planned, all I know is that I have this firm impression that I must enter and remain in an attitude and posture of submission and surrender toward my Lord. I've almost gone from the one end of being bull-headed and charging ahead in everything, to the other end where I'm hesitant to move forward without clear affirmation and confirmation of God's guidance. There is a fear of stepping out of His will and messing things up. I want God to smile too. I want to please His heart.

To view lyrics for songs referenced in this chapter,
please visit http://songdove.fa-ct.com/
There you will find interactive Scripture references, videos containing lyrics to most of the songs listed here, topics mentioned in this chapter, and more.

Scriptures used, referred to or that relate to thoughts in this session:

Psalm 84:10   Joel 2:25

Songs shared, referenced, or that relate to thoughts in this session:

Give it all Away   Foot of the Cross

Topics discussed, referred to, or that relate to thoughts in this session:

Submission/Trust   Obedience, humbleness, surrender
Trust – surrender   Broken – independent spirit
Trust-peace-rest   Brokenness
Gratitude   Dreams and desires
Provision

Questions for Discussion:

What dreams do you have for your life? _____

_____

Have you ever had a dream die? Yes_____ No_____ If yes, did that
dream stay dead or did God revive it?

_____

Who in Scripture had his dreams die, only to be revived in very unexpected
ways? I'll give you a hint, it's one of a few men whose names began with the
letter J.

_____

Ruth, an Example:

In the book of Ruth, the focus of Chapter One is captured in that timeless pledge of commitment found in the second half of the chapter:

> **Ruth 1:16-17** And Ruth said, Intreat me not to leave thee, or to return from following after thee: for whither thou goest, I will go; and where thou lodgest, I will lodge: thy people shall be my people, and thy God my God: ¹⁷Where thou diest, will I die, and there will I be buried: the LORD do so to me, and more also, if ought but death part thee and me.

I found myself asking why I identified with her. The answer didn't come right away, but it occurred to me that the reason I found myself wanting to identify with her is that she is the natural progression for me from what I am learning to be in **Song of Solomon**. **Song of Solomon** taught me the kinds of trials and benefits of choosing to surrender myself and my heart to my King, and Ruth is that actual step of humbleness and submission, of obedience, dedication and commitment, of placing myself at the feet of Jesus and seeking that He put His skirt of marriage over me, humbling myself and surrendering to what may come of such a request and allowing Him to do His part in the process.

When Understanding Breeds Desire:

I don't know if this is something everyone else already knows but I'm only just discovering or what, but I find myself increasingly in a state of desired service and submission toward my unseen Lover, that the more I see and understand of what He did for me and wants to do for me, the deeper this feeling gets. I haven't read the book, "The Five Love Languages", but sometimes I wonder if the two strongest love languages for me are acts of service and words of affirmation. It just seems to be a natural outcropping of my displays of gratitude and appreciation, to both offer words of encouragement and look for ways to give back, usually in acts of service of some form.

I think I'm starting to understand why that admonition by Paul exists in Ephesians where he asks husbands to love their wives and wives to submit to their husbands.

> **Ephesians 5:23-32** For the husband is the head of the wife, even as Christ is the head of the church: and he is the saviour of the body. [24]Therefore as the church is subject unto Christ, so let the wives be to their own husbands in every thing. [25]Husbands, love your wives, even as Christ also loved the church, and gave himself for it; [26]That he might sanctify and cleanse it with the washing of water by the word, [27]That he might present it to himself a glorious church, not having spot, or wrinkle, or any such thing; but that it should be holy and without blemish. [28]So ought men to love their wives as their own bodies. He that loveth his wife loveth himself. [29]For no man ever yet hated his own flesh; but nourisheth and cherisheth it, even as the Lord the church: [30]For we are members of his body, of his flesh, and of his bones. [31]For this cause shall a man leave his father and mother, and shall be joined unto his wife, and they two shall be one flesh. [32]This is a great mystery: but I speak concerning Christ and the church.

Being shown deep-seated, selfless, deeply caring love, protection, provision, and affection, even as intangible as it is coming from God, honestly has me WANTING to submit to Him, wanting to surrender, bowing my head and heart toward Him in a love that really does place myself at His mercy. I see Ruth doing this as she realizes his provision for her as she gleans for Naomi, and as she lays herself at the feet of Boaz, then as she accepts his gift of threshed barley and returns to Naomi to wait out the result of Boaz's actions in the marketplace. Times of discovery, realization, then a humbling willing submission.

I feel this toward God. . . finally learning what it is to desire to surrender my-self to One who has such an incredible love for me. . . *shakes head* I really am such an incredibly late bloomer on all these lessons. But regardless of never having learned them in the human relationship arena, I am finally learn-ing them in the spiritual arena. I can feel the softening in this heart as a result. It's a challenge working out that heart change in life circumstances. I'm still failing various tests that come along to see if I've really indeed changed in certain areas. But my heart is changing, my thought patterns are changing, and eventually those will combine to bring about changes in my words and actions in trying situations.

I looked at that Fruit of the Spirit list again (the reader will find this as a tear-out in this book) and prayed that God would make those things real in my life. . . that His love would reach a point of overflow that would spill into all the areas needing such fruit to be displayed. I don't feel like I'm there yet. Not by a long shot.

Words that came to me that another worship leader felt were worth develop-ing are these on the next page:

Start with me. . .

Let Your Holy Spirit fire burn in me. . .
Let Your flames of love take over till You see. . .

Your love reflected brighter than all the world can offer
Lord Your face seen through my life Lord start with me. . .

Burn in me. . .
May my heart be held wide open, burn through me. . .
May Your flames prepare my life for all to see. . .
May my life reflect Your glory may it tell Salvation's story
Lord may You be lifted wholly, burn in me. . .

All for You. . .
May my heart my soul my mind be all for You. . .
Dedicated to Your purposes that through. . .
This life no longer mine declares the love of Jesus Christ
That I am grafted in the Vine only for You. . .

Come with Me. . .
Child please place your hand in Mine and run with Me. . .
To the peoples and the nations bring to Me. . .
All who suffer in their sin, those caught in Satan's deathly grip
Bring them all let no one slip, come with Me. . .

To view lyrics for songs referenced in this chapter,
please visit http://songdove.fa-ct.com/
There you will find interactive Scripture references, videos containing lyrics to
most of the songs listed here, topics mentioned in this chapter, and more.

Scriptures used, referred to or that relate to thoughts in this session:

Ruth 1: 16-17   Ephesians 5:23-32

Songs shared, referenced, or that relate to thoughts in this session:

Start With Me

Topics discussed, referred to, or that relate to thoughts in this session:

Offering self as an act of worship   Trust-peace-rest
Surrender   Gratitude
Submission/Trust   Pride versus humbleness – willingness
Trust – surrender   Obedience, humbleness, surrender

Questions for Discussion:

What is it about Ruth that make people admire her story so much?

_____

_____

How is marriage typified as a type of relationship with Christ?

_____

_____

Who is easier to respond to?

Someone who is loving, or someone who is distant? _____

_____

Someone who is giving or someone who is demanding? _____

_____

Someone who loves you or someone who hates you? _____

_____

You are the Potter, I am the Clay:

> **Isaiah 64:8** But now, O LORD, thou art our father; we are the clay, and thou our potter; and we all are the work of thy hand.

> **Romans 9:15-21** For he saith to Moses, I will have mercy on whom I will have mercy, and I will have compassion on whom I will have compassion. [16]So then it is not of him that willeth, nor of him that runneth, but of God that sheweth mercy. [17]For the scripture saith unto Pharaoh, Even for this same purpose have I raised thee up, that I might shew my power in thee, and that my name might be declared throughout all the earth. [18]Therefore hath he mercy on whom he will have mercy, and whom he will he hardeneth. [19]Thou wilt say then unto me, Why doth he yet find fault? For who hath resisted his will? [20]Nay but, O man, who art thou that repliest against God? Shall the thing formed say to him that formed it, Why hast thou made me thus? [21]Hath not the potter power over the clay, of the same lump to make one vessel unto honour, and another unto dishonour?

> **Malachi 3:3** And he shall sit as a refiner and purifier of silver: and he shall purify the sons of Levi, and purge them as gold and silver, that they may offer unto the LORD an offering in righteousness.

Can the clay tell the potter how they wish to be shaped? Can the gold and silver tell the smith how they wish to be purified? . . . Talk about submission, surrender. . . my head and heart bow just thinking about it. . . I want the passion, the intimacy, the closeness. To close up on God because I don't want the refining is to also shut out His presence. . . I don't, can't, shut Him out after how He's shown Himself to me. . .

Only God knows where He's taking me, but . . . wow. . . that's almost all I can say as I look at what is happening to me. Can a person be any more a bundle of seeming contradictions than I am? If I listen to my choir songs correctly, even my bouts of loneliness are tools in God's hands, as unpleasant as they are, making me appreciate His presence increasingly as each bout hits me. He is certainly a God of adventure! Once again I have to say that anyone who tries to say Christianity is boring, hasn't met my life! If God can be doing this much in a hermit's life, imagine what He can do with someone who has more social skills?

The desire refreshes in my mind to be open to His hand, to be surrendered to His ultimate will, to allow myself to be completely taken over by His love, by His Holy Spirit, no matter how many ouch moments I may end up with as time goes by. Such desires renew the need to allow myself to be broken to be used of Him, to achieve His purposes and to bring glory to Him rather than try to "get it right", and "perfect myself" before God can use me in His Kingdom.

It doesn't seem to matter what the initial thought is, but that surrender and submission don't somehow work their way into it. I can't get away from the fact that nothing happens of any lasting consequence in the heart, spirit and mind of the Christian apart from surrender to the Holy Spirit and submission to His will. It seems to be a thread through everything I am encountering. First God introduced Himself as my unseen Lover, and I am now realizing anew, realizing with my heart this time instead of just my head, that the Lover of my Soul longs for me to surrender myself to Him, that as I allow myself to be permeated with His love, as I submit to the changing transformation His love is working within me, that I will in turn spread that love to those around me via the Fruit of the Spirit.

God's Love Shown Through Broken Vessels:

> **Psalm 34:18** The LORD *is* nigh unto them that are of a broken heart; and saveth such as be of a contrite spirit.

> **Psalm 147:3** He healeth the broken in heart, and bindeth up their wounds.

I now know how to show God's love to the world around me. I need to continually surrender myself, continually submit myself to the King of Kings and to the love He longs to show me. . . I need to continually allow that searchlight to cleanse me, to remove every dark thing that is revealed, and to make me fit for service in His Kingdom. A service that God has shown me is most easily done through the broken life, through the cracked clay pot, because those cracks are in God's eyes, beautiful black lines in the marble that makes up this living stone. As I allow myself to be gently broken under the power of His amazingly passionate, intimate love, He will take my broken shards and form me into the person He desires me to be for the purposes He has fashioned for me and in so doing touch the world around me.

To read Scriptures referenced in this chapter,
please visit http://songdove.fa-ct.com/
There you will find interactive Scripture references, videos containing lyrics to most of the songs in these chapters, topics mentioned in this chapter, and more.

Scriptures used, referred to or that relate to thoughts in this session:

Isaiah 64:8	Psalm 147:3
Romans 9:15-21	Ezekiel 34:16
Malachi 3:3	Matthew 21:44
Ephesians 5:23-32	Habakkuk 3:17-19
Psalm 34:18	Job 13:15
Psalm 51:8, 17	Isaiah 40:31

Topics discussed, referred to, or that relate to thoughts in this session:

Offering self as an act of worship   Gratitude
Surrender   Willingness
Forgiveness   Obedience, humbleness, surrender
Unknown – change, fear   Broken – independent spirit
Submission/Trust   Brokenness
Trust – surrender   Remain open during trials and tests
Trust-peace-rest

Questions for Discussion:

What does it mean to be clay in the potter's hand? _____

_____

From the verses listed here, why is it necessary to for one to willingly be broken before God?

_____

_____

What is happening when God refines a person?   Hint, look at the previous study session for a passage in Ephesians. . .

_____

_____

Rest involves peace which involves trust

Rest involves peace which involves trust, a correlation that didn't hit me until that month of sudden discovery of God's deeply personal love for me. I still feel late to the table on this, but I've come and while I'm still having to learn to rest with the lack of answers occasionally, I'm learning to trust. I dare not say I've arrived on this issue or some test will show up to see if I really have learned this lesson.

> **Habakkuk 3:17-19** Although the fig tree shall not blossom, neither shall fruit be in the vines; the labour of the olive shall fail, and the fields shall yield no meat; the flock shall be cut off from the fold, and there shall be no herd in the stalls: [18]Yet I will rejoice in the LORD, I will joy in the God of my salvation. [19]The LORD God is my strength, and he will make my feet like hinds' feet, and he will make me to walk upon mine high places. To the chief singer on my stringed instruments.

> **Job 13:14-16** Wherefore do I take my flesh in my teeth, and put my life in mine hand? [15]Though he slay me, yet will I trust in him: but I will maintain mine own ways before him. [16]He also shall be my salvation: for an hypocrite shall not come before him.

To reach a point of those last few verses of Habakkuk is to reach a point of total surrender to God's perfect ways and total submission to His perfect will in our lives. . . to say with Job that though He slay me, yet will I trust Him. . . and amazingly, to find Joy in the midst of that. It's as if there is a deep lightness of the inner man in the middle of trials and struggles that only God can give when we trust Him implicitly. Like that of a sleeping child unaware of the road conditions, like a toddler unaware of the stock market fluctuations.

Unlike both those examples, we are well aware, and yet, in spite of our aware-ness of our corner of the big picture, if God has our total, unquestioning, implicit trust in all our life's circumstances, there is this promise of content-ment, of Joy that comes in the middle of our circumstances.

> **Isaiah 40:28-31** Hast thou not known? hast thou not heard, that the everlasting God, the LORD, the Creator of the ends of the earth, fainteth not, neither is weary? there is no searching of his understanding. [29]He giveth power to the faint; and to them that have no might he increaseth strength. [30]Even the youths shall faint and be weary, and the young men shall utterly fall: [31]But they that wait upon the LORD shall renew their strength; they shall mount up with wings as eagles; they shall run, and not be weary; and they shall walk, and not faint.

I've mused occasionally about the difference between soaring on wings as eagles, rising above our circumstances, and the eye of the storm, peace in the middle of our hurricane of life. . . When do we rise and when do we find that place of peace as the wind swirls around us. . . that is a curiosity. But Scrip-ture speaks of both ways of handling what life throws at us, and regardless of which analogy works best for us, both involve trust, peace, and rest in God's loving care of us.

Fulfillment. . . in the resting or the doing? . . . or neither? A bit of a di-version, but still on the topic of surrender, God's plans for our lives, etc.

This thought comes to me as I have been becoming more aware of several as-pects of life that all end up balling together in my mind. 1) Who we are, what we think we are, our identity, where we find it, 2) Busyness, 3)Rest

One thought that got me musing about these issues was a conversation about identity. There was concern that finding one's identity based on what they did or the role they played in the church would narrow their focus too much and cause problems in the future. I see two sides to that particular coin. . .

1) The side where the person loses all sense of who they are if they are not busy about God's House.
2) The side where the person learns, matures, and grows in God's House as young Samuel did, and goes out from there with a confidence they would not have had elsewhere.

My family fits into the second category, that is, my siblings and I. I don't joke when I say we "lived" at the church when I was younger. If people who share this concern saw how often my brother was here during a week, they'd have been more worried about him than about many others. Yet as I shared at one meeting, he took the training he received at my church, and went on to use it professionally in Alberta for several years. Since then he's achieved his electrical apprenticeship but still does a major youth convention known as YC every year, still "living" at church, etc.

It's possible for others to be trained and brought to maturity within a church's four walls and then sent out just like my brother was. I tell my children that if they can't learn something at home, it will be far harder to learn it out in the world, and I believe the same is true of the church family. If we can't learn something "at home", it will be that much harder out in the world. In the case of technical training the "harder" part is often in the form of student loan debts racked up to get the same training they would have received in God's House. There may be other dangers too from learning in the world versus learning in the church, such as falling in with the wrong crowd, losing one's faith to a hard-line professor, etc.

There are people who need to be raised in the hothouse of God's love in order to be strong enough to withstand life outside. Others can handle it, they have the personality and determination that no one will shake them.

But for people like my son, NOT wrapping them in the cocoon of God's Love for awhile has meant falling-away for many years, and for some of those who fall away, they never return to the faith. Eventually it is desired that such people will become strong enough in their faith such that branching into pursuits outside the church will not be as detrimental to their faith as it could be otherwise.

My siblings and I were never classified as weak personalities. But even we benefited from "living" at the church in our younger years, and my brother and I have never really let go of that concept in our own lives. My desires died along with my divorce for several years prior to being discovered, but with healing and restoration has come revival of these desires for God's House and I too, would be there much more than I am if daily life allowed it.

Personally, there is room for being found within protective walls for those who need that protection while their faith matures.

The person loses all sense of who they are

Point One) in this section is something I see in the secular world too, not just the Church. People who lose all sense of who they are when the kids leave home, or who lose their identity when they get fired from a job, or who aren't happy unless they are at work, at school or on the court. They aren't what they do, but they think they are. At times we all need to ask ourselves. . . "who am I if I can no longer be found doing this or that?" In this respect I'm glad for the varied nature of my interests, talents and giftings God has given me. I'm a singer, a computer tech, a web master, a mother, a former biker, a writer, a prayer warrior. . . the list could go on with likes and dislikes, etc. But if I couldn't sing, if I couldn't fix computers anymore, if the kids left home and I couldn't write anymore, I am still a Child of God. That is where my identity lies. I'd fight feelings of uselessness for sure, but only until God revealed to me what I could do next.

Whether we grab our identity from the church, or from our workplace, school or recreational pursuit, our ultimate identity is found in Christ, and that is the message we need to impart to the young ones coming up in ministry. We are their safe place, their safe training ground, their refuge until they are ready to take on the world as solid members of the faith.

There is a place for shelter, and a place for exposure. I think some such as my son, and others who may come up after them of that mindset and faith-place, need the shelter of the church for a time in their lives.

It is my prayer they will one day find their wings and fly free like my brother did, knowing they are welcome to return to the nest as often as they want.

Indeed who are we when we are not busy doing the things we love? As I stated previously, sometimes people really do grab their identity from their job, their sport, their volunteer involvement, their family status, etc. Many people have written articles and books, and delivered speeches and sermons about the dangers of being busy in today's North American society.

Busy has most definitely become the Christian's worst enemy! But telling the Christian to slow down when they grab their identity from what keeps them busy is like telling them to lose all sense of who they are. We've all heard various cliches such as "being so busy for God that we have no time to spend with God", "being so heavenly minded we are no earthly good", "too busy to pray", etc. But until we address the issue of who we are apart from what we do, these cliches will continue to be true of many of us.

To read Scriptures referenced in this chapter,
please visit http://songdove.fa-ct.com/
There you will find interactive Scripture references, videos containing lyrics to most of the songs in these chapters, topics mentioned in this chapter, and more.

Scriptures used, referred to or that relate to thoughts in this session:

Habakkuk 3:17-19   Isaiah 40:31
Job 13:15

Topics discussed, referred to, or that relate to thoughts in this session:

Submission/Trust   Letting God live through us
Trust – surrender   Remain open during trials and tests
Trust-peace-rest   Who I am in Christ
Obedience, humbleness, surrender

Questions for Discussion:

What three words characterize the heart and position of the submitted life?

_____

On the companion website, on the chapter 4 page, there is a link there called "Who I am in Christ". If you can't get to the website, grab a reference Bible such Thompson-Chain, to look up this topic in their topics section. Take some time to review this list and make two notes:

1) Note those verses you firmly believe are true of your position in Christ.

_____

_____

2) Note those verses you aren't so sure apply to you. Ask yourself why, Ask God why, and see what He reveals to you.

_____

_____

Who Are You?

I had a short daydream (yes, this author is a dreamer) as I was loading the washing machine one day. I'm one of those people happiest when I'm busy doing things in, around, or for God's House and the Kingdom of God, whether it's directly church-related, or inter-church-related. But I'm also one of those people who will deliberately take a "do-nothing" day when I sense myself getting too tired to carry on. Today was to be an "almost do-nothing" day, as some of the more pressing chores still needed to get done, but I needed a day to just relax!

These thoughts were going around my head as I began the load of wash and this daydream hit. In this daydream, I'd been forced against my will into a room where I couldn't even do the things I enjoy when relaxing. All that was in this room was a bed, a chair and a bedside table.

Then I heard God say, or rather rhetorically ask, "Who are you?"

The first answer that popped out of my mouth, in spite of everything God's been teaching me about learning to live life as the Bride of Christ, was "your servant Lord".

I could almost sense God shaking His head as He asked again, "Who are you?"

My second answer was "Your daughter".

That answer pleased Him a little more, I could sense that, but He replied, "You are more than that my child, who are you?"

As I recall this, I am bowing my heart as my final answer, and the answer that ended the daydream was this, "I am your bride, and one day, at the marriage supper of the Lamb, I will become your wife, and will reign with You".

We can find fulfilment, satisfaction and pleasure in the doing of life, in the serving and giving and activity found in putting God's purposes and desires into action for our churches and communities, but who we are is not found in those pursuits, as beneficial and enjoyable as they may be.

I sit here in a little bit of chagrin as I realize my first answer was the wrong answer. It wasn't wrong from the perspective that we are called "servants of the Most High", bond-slaves to Jesus Christ, etc, in the Scriptures, but wrong in that it is only part of the total answer, it is not the final, complete answer!

Our Position in Christ

The final, complete answer is found in our position in Christ, that of being members of His Bride. Christ even modelled the serving, giving nature that a husband is supposed to have toward his wife, to the point of laying down His life for His Bride on the Cross of Calvary! In the same way, we are to be so in love with Christ, so in love with Jesus that we will serve Him to the point of laying our own lives down for Him in return! We are not servants with a distant, untouchable master. We are not merely children with chores to do in the house, but we are destined as the corporate Bride, chosen by God the Father for God the Son and witnessed by God the Holy Spirit, with John the Baptist testifying to this event early in the Gospel of John, as "Friend of the Bridegroom" according to Jewish tradition.

Our service, no matter how busy we get, must never be out of duty, duress, or the search or maintenance of personal identity, but out of an unquenchable desire to bring a smile to the face of the eternal Lover of our Souls! To sense His smile beats out all the financial remuneration this world can offer! To feel His embrace and the pleasure in His heart toward us is something we will never get anywhere else!

We are brought into the family of God, not as servants, but as children of the Most High God. He cleans us up and presents us to His Son as the Bride of Christ! Christ came to us washing feet, feeding the hungry, healing the sick, raising the dead, forgiving sins. His identity was not in what He did, but in who He was, as God the Son, second of this mystery we call the Trinity, seeking to honour His Father in Heaven, and court His future Bride, issuing "her" the Jewish rite of betrothal at what we now call The Last Supper.

Therefore we should serve, not at a distance, but out of love, a deeply grateful responding love for the One who gave His life for us! We have been rescued for His glory and for His pleasure. We are His! Our identity is found in Christ and Christ alone!

So if our identity is not found in what we do but in Christ, this leaves the challenge of learning to truly rest! To just stop what we're doing for awhile, and rest, actually "take 5", take a few deep breaths, and relax! Rest in Christ. Christ asks us to come to Him and find rest for our souls. My daughter brought me Matthew 11:28-30 one night.

> **Matthew 11:28-30** Come unto me, all ye that labour and are heavy laden, and I will give you rest. 29Take my yoke upon you, and learn of me; for I am meek and lowly in heart: and ye shall find rest unto your souls. 30For my yoke is easy, and my burden is light.

So many of us are so busy doing, that rest is a threat to us. The thought of slowing down and doing nothing for awhile literally comes as a threat to some people. Just like the concept of silence. Some people have to have the TV or radio going because they can't handle the silence.

Other than finding our identity in what we do instead of in who we are in Christ, I think the other major reason for people refusing to slow down and rest, is that resting, being in a state of quietness, causes the mind to relax, and in that relaxed state, things come to the fore of our minds that we really don't want to think about.

I know for myself that I've just about cursed some of those times. I'd go to relax in silence and discover all these thoughts coming forward that I really didn't want to deal with. Painful emotions, memories, situations and what seemed worse yet, God actually wanted to deal with those things Himself!

Staying busy was a way to avoid those moments. I began to realize however, that if I just let God do His thing, if I listened to the voices of those God brought into my life and just rested in my lack of answers, that God was about to engage in an incredible amount of healing and restoration in my life. I'd been hiding from dealing with the issues that would haunt me in the quiet moments for several years. But I couldn't hide anymore.

Now, a few years after I was forced to start facing these things, I embrace the quiet times. Rest doesn't seem so threatening to me as it once was and I am finding that God wants to share those quiet moments with me. I have to say that there is no better way to quiet the anxious heart than to let God wrap His arms around you! That 360 degree hug that I've come to know is so quieting, so peaceful, so assuring, or reassuring as the need might be at the time.

God wants relationship with us, both as His children, and as the Bride of Christ. Some of us relate better to God the Father, while more and more of us are starting to wake up to God the Son desiring relationship with His Bride. The past few years have seen me begin my own journey into this rela-tionship, and again, those moments of intimacy where God's heart touches mine, where my spirit touches His, can only happen in stillness, in moments of rest.

When you think about it, how many married couples say they are happy when they are so busy doing that they have no time for each other intimately? No time to just sit and share moments of nothing more than just being in each other's presence, sometimes held in an embrace, sometimes talking, some-times silent, but together. . . Our relationship with God is no different. We will never fully discover the deep love God has for us if we are so busy doing that we don't take time to just "be" with Him.

God longs for us to allow ourselves to be vulnerable in those restful moments. Let Him work. Let Him heal. Let Him restore. Let Him bring us to wholeness. He will send us out in His due time, asking if we will be willing to do various things that are close to His heart and I have to say, the closer we get to His heart, the more we discover the kinds of activities that bring Him the most pleasure. Those activities are directly related to reaching out into the world around us and touching it with the love of Christ, healing the sick, feeding the hungry, bringing Christ's salvation and offer of forgiveness so that as many as possible can come to Him and begin their own relationship with the One who died for them.

We must never get so busy that we lose our identity in our busyness. We must never get so busy that we fear the restful quiet times. We are the Bride of Christ, and He longs to spend time with us! Just us! Spirit to spirit and Heart to heart. . . Therein lies true fulfilment. . .

To read Scriptures referenced in this chapter,
please visit http://songdove.fa-ct.com/
There you will find interactive Scripture references, videos containing lyrics to
most of the songs in these chapters, topics mentioned in this chapter, and
more.

Scriptures used, referred to or that relate to thoughts in this session:

Ephesians 5:23-32   Matthew 11: 28-30

Topics discussed, referred to, or that relate to thoughts in this session:

Submission/Trust	Obedience, humbleness, surrender
Trust – surrender	Letting God live through us
Trust-peace-rest	Remain open during trials and tests
Gratitude	Who I am in Christ
Provision	Servanthood

Questions for Discussion:

Who does Scripture say you are? _____

_____

What kinds of behaviour characterizes a member of the Body and Bride of Christ?

_____

_____

Looking back over these study sessions, what words would you use to describe the lessons in this section? (IE: surrender, peace, trust)

_____

_____

Personal notes:

_____

_____

_____

Proof

Made in the USA
Charleston, SC
28 July 2012